SCOTTISH BATTLES

Malcolm Archibald

Chambers

Published 1990 by W & R Chambers Ltd,
43-45 Annandale Street, Edinburgh EH7 4AZ

British Library Cataloguing in Publication Data
Archibald, Malcolm
  Scottish battles.
  1. Scotland. Battles
  I. Title
  941.1

ISBN 0-550-20060-6

Acknowledgement

I am indebted to W K Moncur Esq, and Group Captain
Denholm, both ex-603 Squadron, for their invaluable
help in the details of the German raid of 16 October
1939.

Illustrations by John Haxby and Janet MacKay
Cover design by John Marshall

Typeset by Bookworm Typesetting Ltd, Edinburgh
Printed in Singapore by
Singapore National Printers Ltd

Contents

Preface

There have been many battles in Scotland and this book contains only a limited selection. Fifteen battles are presented, each unique. They are given in five sections: English wars, civil and clan wars, religious wars, Jacobite wars and finally an air battle against Germany over the Forth.

Bannockburn, first of the English battles, was fought by Robert Bruce. Halidon was lost to that English phenomenon, the longbow. Flodden displayed the faults and virtues of one of the better Stuart kings, James IV, Solway Moss proved to be the folly of the royal favourite, Oliver Sinclair. Ancrum is included to exhibit the strange habits of the Scottish nobility – and the skill of her spearmen.

The second section starts with Red Harlaw when Clan Donald declared war on Lowland Scotland, continues with the galley fight of Bloody Bay which began the disintegration of the Gaelic west, and ends with Langside where Mary, Queen of Scots, was defeated.

Religious wars dominated Scotland for a century, and Inverlochy is one of the best remembered of Montrose's victories. It also illustrates the downfall of the Gael. Three decades later Covenanters faced Bluidy Clavers at Drumclog, with their Church as a prize.

Then came the Jacobites. Their romantic image has become enshrined as part of Scotland's heritage. Romantic? Consider the result of a claymore's sweep at Killiecrankie, the spiralling battle of Sherrifmuir or the five-minute fight of Prestonpans. There was surely no romance at Culloden.

Friends after years of emnity, Scots and English combined to face a continental enemy in Hitler in the Second World War and over the Forth the aircraft of both nations met.

ENGLISH WARS

Bannockburn

For 18 years war had flared over Scotland but now it would end; it had to. With such forces arrayed against them, the tiny Scottish army could not win. Rank after rank, the might of England uncoiled along the high road to Stirling. Three thousand heavy cavalry led the way. They were the élite, the prime fighting force who would smash their way through any defence. Feudal warfare was built around the armoured knight with his great charger, his sword and his head-crushing lance. These men had been trained to fight since boyhood; it was their purpose in life.

Behind the knights marched 15000 footmen. To most medieval armies the infantry merely made up the numbers, but the English were different. Much more important than either spearmen or men-at-arms, the longbowmen moved with an arrogant knowledge of their own skill. Already the Scots knew that they should be wary of them; Wallace's spear rings at Falkirk had been destroyed by the hail of yard-long arrows. Not only English archers, but also Welsh, boasted of carrying twelve men's lives in their belts; watching their inexorable progress, the Scots knew this to be true. Scotland had nothing to match the range and penetrating power of Edward's archers.

What the Scots did have was experience and leadership. Experience gained in nearly two decades of unremitting warfare, the leadership of Robert Bruce who had risen to be King, of James Douglas, the Good Sir James who was victor of a dozen encounters, of Randolph Moray who had recently captured Edinburgh Castle, of fiery Edward Bruce who once won a battle by leading 50 men in a charge on 1500. The Scots also knew they were fighting for their own country, not on feudal demand. They fought because they wanted to fight.

There were few armoured knights in the Scottish host and perhaps 500 mounted men all told; few could compare on level terms with heavy cavalry. The remainder of the Scots were infantry: Lowland spearmen or Highland sworders, men of Galloway or part-Norse Hebrideans. With their short bows, the archers from the Ettrick Forest could not fire as far as the English, but in a close fight they could be just as accurate. In all there were maybe 5000 Scots.

At their head was Robert Bruce, crowned King at Scone seven years before and a fugitive shortly after. An intelligent fighting man, he hacked his way to power with his sword. Bruce would be a worried man, for set-piece battles were not his style. Lacking both the equipment and numbers of the English, Bruce preferred his Scots to fight as guerrillas, a method of warfare their temperament and the nature of the country favoured. Now a rash challenge had forced him into conventional battle.

In medieval warfare, castles were all-important. They held garrisons, subdued the surrounding area, provided bases for armies and a bastion for defence. Scotland was studded with strategic strongholds, and Stirling was central to the state. Situated at the lowest bridging point of the Forth, and where the Lowland plain was joined to the Highlands, Stirling was the padlock which held Scotland secure. The key to this lock was the castle; hold the castle and hazard all north-south communications. This was no secret: Scots and English had battled for years to keep Stirling Castle.

There had been a siege of the English-held castle, but the Scots had made no impression on the rock-set fortress, so they made an agreement instead. Unless the castle was relieved by midsummer's day 1314 – in a year's time – the garrison would surrender. As this was not an uncommon arrangement for this period, and gave them twelve months' grace, the English agreed.

Now it was the eve of midsummer 1314 and Edward

II had brought his army to relieve Stirling. To keep his prestige and Scots morale, Bruce had to meet and defeat the English.

No fool, Bruce attempted to equalise the odds. He chose a battlefield with ground too soft for the English cavalry, with a wood – Torwood – at his back in case of retreat, with the New Park for closer cover and the Bannock Burn trickling between formidable banks in the centre.

Between the foliage of the New Park and the Bannock Burn, Bruce made his men hack pits. Camouflaging them with branches, Bruce had made a trap for cavalry. Added to this were caltrops, four pronged spikes which could impale the hooves of horses or the feet of careless men.

The Scots were formed into four spear rings between the boggy Carse of Stirling and Torwood. Cavalry could not penetrate the spears, but the closely packed infantry provided a perfect target for archers.

Randolph commanded the extreme left, then Walter the Steward and Douglas; Edward Bruce led the third and Robert Bruce stood firm on the banks of the burn. Keith, the Marischal, commanded the cavalry while a few archers were in the New Park.

As rumours of the English advance reached the ranks, Bruce stated that any man could leave at that time and not be thought a coward. None left; there were old scores to settle with the English.

The English advanced with the Earls of Gloucester and Hereford in the vanguard. Unable to hold them, the Ettrick archers withdrew, encouraging the English knights into a galloping charge. Lances thrust out, helmeted heads forward and hooves thudding the sodden ground, the leading knights would hardly see the lone horseman in their path. It was Robert Bruce.

On a pony and with a light axe for defence, Bruce faced the leading knight, one Henry de Bohun. Heavily armoured, Bohun could charge only in a straight line, and Bruce outmanoeuvred him, hefted his battle-axe and clove the Englishman's skull. First blood to the Scots, and the English were among the pits and caltrops, taking casualties among the screaming fury of shattered horses. The English withdrew but another, potentially more dangerous, movement began.

Sir Robert Clifford led 300 knights over the Carse, but Randolph's spearmen were sent to block their road to the castle. A stubborn mêlée ensued, cavalry against spearmen and the cavalry were forced to withdraw. Elated but exhausted, the spearmen rested on their weapons; for the day's fighting had ended.

There was nowhere for the English to camp but on the Carse. There was water, and the cheering sight of the leopard banner above Stirling Castle. Unfortunately, the soft ground was unsuitable for heavy cavalry. It would be a tense night with the Scots outnumbered, the English crowded and wet.

An early mass followed by a bread and water breakfast and the Scots advanced on the bog-juggling English. Spears and leather against plate armour and packed thousands; the Scots looked too puny to fight. They advanced across the Carse but halted, perhaps to dress their ranks, maybe to receive a final blessing but Edward II thought they pleaded for mercy. There was to be little mercy that day.

With limited space, the English could not gather sufficient momentum for a proper charge; their cavalry failed on the Scottish spears. Gloucester died here, and hundreds more as the Scots pressed forward their spears. Compressed into an ever more restricted area, the battle became a squalid, muddy killing match with frustrated knights hurling lances and ragged Scots soldiers probing long spears into man and horse alike.

For a minute Edward of England broke the deadlock as his archers found high ground and hissing shafts plunged into unprotected spearmen, but Keith had the answer. Scots chivalry had no reputation at all before this battle and very little in fights to come, but here the Marischal led them into a slashing charge which scattered the archers it did not kill.

With that threat removed, Bruce threw in his Highland reserve and the claymore and dirk sliced into English armour. But the fight could still go either way: the Scots were tiring and if they broke the English cavalry would roll them up. There were no reserves left to call on, but the massed English foot could not get into contact for their own knights; they began to drift away.

With more room to move, the cavalry turned their horses, the whole line shivered and 'On them!' the Scots are said to have yelled, 'On them, they fail!'

With that, the camp followers joined in. 'Upon them now! They shall all die!' and perhaps this little reinforcement helped for the English broke and ran.

Edward II, with an escort of 500, was one of the first away. He fled to Dunbar, took a ship to safety and let his escort hack their own way clear. Knights and lords were captured for ransom, though 35 English nobles were dead, with over 200 knights and 700 lesser gentry. The common English dead were never counted — nor the Scots, although only three Scots knights died.

Stirling fell to Robert Bruce but the war continued.

Halidon Hill

After Bannockburn the Scots were in the ascendancy under the mantle of Bruce and Douglas. In 1320 the people of Scotland signed the Declaration of Arbroath, which stated both their continued desire for freedom and their intention of removing any King who sold their freedom to the English. That declaration remains the most important document in Scottish history. It was not long before the Scots had to prove their beliefs.

Peace came with the Treaty of Edinburgh and two years later Bruce was dead. Randolph Moray and Douglas followed shortly after, and Edward Bruce had died in an Irish battle some years before. Scotland lay open to English invasion. With an anglicised Balliol at their head, an army of English and disinherited Scots landed in Fife. They defeated a Scots army at Dupplin near Perth and crowned Balliol as Edward, King of Scots.

The new King did not remain long in the north. With the patriots retaking Perth, Balliol scurried for safety to the English Border, promised homage to Edward III and attempted to rule his kingdom from Annan. And from Annan he was driven away.

During a scrambled fight at midnight in a wet December, swords crossed once again and Balliol, near naked, fled on a barebacked horse. Another Douglas was regent, Archibald, brother of the Good Sir James, and the Scots followed their success by a raid over the border. Until now a supposedly secret supporter, Edward III decided to aid Balliol directly.

Small-scale warfare flickered on the frontier, with the English normally victorious, and Balliol made a tentative return to Roxburgh Castle. In the meantime Edward III raised an army and laid siege to Berwick.

At one time Berwick had been the most important port in Scotland, but two generations of war had altered the town's status to a significant frontier fortress. Berwick was to change hands eleven times before settling on the English side of the border.

The Earl of March, not noted for his patriotism, held Berwick Castle for Scotland while Sir Alexander Seton held the town. Both were heartened by news of Scots warships wasting the seaports of England.

Edward ignored this detail and used his fleet to block-ade Berwick. The siege followed a familiar pattern: a foray by the defenders brought fire to the pitch and timber English shipping, an English assault across the ditch, stuffed with bundles of sticks, was repulsed and the attackers fell back to try starvation. This was more effective: town and castle weakened as supplies slowly dwindled. As with Stirling 20 years before, an arrangement was made: if the town was not relieved by a certain date it would surrender. To encourage the defenders to keep their word – for a knight's honour was not always to be trusted – the English took some hostages.

It was the Bannockburn situation in reverse. This time the Scots had to find an army to raise the siege; the English were to prevent them. By high summer Regent Douglas was ready. His army marched south, arrogant after a generation of victory, forgetful of the lesson of Dupplin Moor where English archers had whittled the Scots like chaff.

Chronicles quote incredible numbers: 20 000 would be a high estimate but not an impossible one. When the hungry folk of Berwick saw the regent's force splash through the Yare Ford, circle round the town and clatter close, they shouted their relief and exhilaration.

No cautious commander, Douglas forced forward a strong body of men under Sir William Keith to reinforce the town. A fierce fight in the skirmish lines, sword to sword and the war-cries of chivalry but Keith's men smashed through. Technically the town had been relieved but Edward III refused to move. For a full 36 hours the two armies glared at each other, neither pre-pared to attack, then Douglas decided to draw the Eng-lish. Leading his men south, he menaced Bamburgh, where the English Queen was residing.

Edward was not to be drawn; on the contrary he demanded Berwick's surrender as the Scots army had disappeared without entering the town. The besieged refused, pointing out that Keith had got through and was now their new governor. It seemed like an impasse, but Edward promptly hanged one of his hostages, Thomas Seton, son of the ex-governor, in view of the towns-folk.

Naturally there was concern among the citizens – some of their sons were being held hostage too. They remembered an earlier siege of Berwick when Edward

9

I had massacred a good part of the population. Surrender seemed sensible – and Keith was persuaded. Unless 200 Scots entered Berwick by 19 July, or the regent's army defeated the English, he would surrender.

In fairness to Keith, his intention was to force Douglas to defeat the English. Berwick was the lure for both armies. Unfortunately, Douglas agreed. If he had waited, the English army might have disintegrated; for there were already murmurings in that direction. As it was, Douglas led his men back across the Tweed.

With months to scout the ground, Edward had chosen his battlefield with care. He brought his army to Halidon Hill, which was 500 feet high and a couple of miles north-west of Berwick. He then posted them on the northern slope in three divisions and waited confidently.

He had reason to be confident: he had found a good position for his men, he had equal numbers and thousands of archers. Here was the cream of the English army, strong men clad in deerskin with bows of yew as tall as themselves, strung with flax or silk. Their arrows were made of steel-tipped oak and had goose wings to guide them. Between the archers were spearmen, behind them were the armoured knights.

French wars were to bring fame to English bowmen, but they perfected their craft in Scotland. It took a Bruce or a James Douglas to counter the missile storm of England. In the forthcoming battle the Scots had neither.

The regent was a poor copy of his brother and his dispositions were a poor copy of Bruce's army at Bannockburn. Four divisions, each led by a famous name: Archibald Douglas led one; 17-year-old Steward II led the second; the Earl of Moray, son of the hero of Edinburgh Castle, led the third; and the Earl of Ross the last. It was 19 July 1333 and the hot sun beat upon the Scots host as they trudged through bogland at the foot of Halidon Hill. There would have been cursing and sliding, the inevitable confusion of inexperienced troops and perhaps defiant shouts at the distant English.

As the Scots advanced, they became aware of a disturbing phenomenon: men were falling, feathered shafts penetrating their leather-protected bodies. The Scots would have hurried, struggling against the slime and mud to close with their enemy and all the time the arrows fell. The closer the Scots reached, the more accurate the English fire. Confusion continued among the ensuing death. English trumpets blasted tauntingly and still the Scots were scores of yards short.

With faces averted from the killing hail of arrows and already with some Highlanders hesitating, the spearmen advanced grimly, defiantly, hopelessly into the affray. Bravery was not enough; as they cleared the bog the Scots could run at last. Spears raining down on them they bounded upward, gasping, at the invulnerable English. But they soon became tired; with formations forgotten they faced an unbroken line of English spears. For a while the two sides surged in close combat but only a handful of Scots had reached the summit and now the English cavalry slid from the flanks.

With no tight spear ring to oppose them, the cavalry were in their element. Axe and mace, sword and lance were used against scattered footsoldiers. The Scots infantry broke and fled. All that courage could do they had done, but ill-led and badly armed they had fought unavailingly. At the end, the Earl of Ross made a last desperate attack, leading the remnants of his Highlanders against Balliol's wing. Like the others, this effort failed and the slope of Halidon was the scene of a massacre.

Archibald Douglas was captured, too wounded to resist. He was to die in captivity. Five other earls died, and 70 barons, hundreds of knights and gentlemen. Nobody bothered to count the spearmen but an estimate of 14 000 Scots dead was given – 1000 for every admitted English casualty.

The victory at Bannockburn had been reversed and the English thought that Scotland lay open before them. By their lights, it did; for there was no nobility left alive to raise an army.

The results were catastrophic for Scotland. Balliol returned with the disinherited and the English ruled by pulling the strings of their puppet King. With one set of leaders dead, another rose through the ranks, men who proved better suited to the Scots style of fighting. Warfare raged through the nation and England learned once again that they could defeat a Scots army, they could occupy the land, but they would never be able to defeat the people. For in defeat the Scots remained ever defiant.

Flodden

A handful of miles over the Border, a stark stone pillar squats amid the sodden grass. It is nothing, a lump of stone to mark another battle between Scots and English, yet here was fought one of the bloodiest-ever fights between the two nations. Here died one of Scotland's proudest kings, here was broken the Cheshire Division and here the flower of Scotland died with steel bills thrust through their still advancing bodies.

There had been peace along the frontier. For a generation no major army had crossed the hills of Cheviot nor sullied Tweed with the passage of armed men. After two centuries of war Scotland was a poor country of gaunt fortresses and a population more used to hefting a spear than dealing with trade. There was a potential for culture shown in the Border ballads and the tremendous oral tradition of the Gaels, but it was not until the reign of James IV that this potential was realised. With James' encouragement the Renaissance prospered in Scotland but with his impetuosity he dropped the country into a period as bleak as any in Scotland's history.

The story of James IV is indeed a Scottish tragedy. Handsome and clever, James introduced compulsory education for his monied subjects, chartered Edinburgh's College of Surgeons and inspired a generation of poets. More importantly for his subjects' peace of mind, James took an English Queen and there were hopes that their offspring would rule both nations. Perhaps there would be an end to warfare and farmers on both sides of Cheviot could plant their fields with an expectation of reaping a full crop.

Unfortunately these high hopes were a full century early. The natural character of both nations was still primed to aggression and Border raiding never seemed to halt. This produced a measure of tension, as did an outbreak of English naval piracy, but it needed a third power to produce open warfare from this minor skirmishing. As so often, France acted as catalyst and a woman, in the form of Louis XII's wife, added the finishing touch.

Outwith the British Isles, Europe was a composition of alliances. Pope and Holy Roman Empire combined against France, and Henry VIII of England rolled on to the bandwagon. Henry was another English King who turned a terrible face towards Scotland, but first Scotland turned against him. Reading his man correctly, Louis XII of France appealed to James' boyish chivalry. Anne of Brittany, Louis' Queen, sent a personal request for James' help, informed him he was her champion and enclosed a turquoise finger ring as proof of her trust. That aluminium copper phosphate was to cause immeasurable loss to Scotland, for it convinced romantic James he had to act.

If the Scots King had been cautious as well as unwise there might still have been a chance, but James had the Scots fault of headstrong bravery mingled with a notion of chivalry more suited to *Mort d'Arthur* than to a Renaissance prince. Furthering his distance from Henry, James formed an alliance with an Irish O'Donnell and fitted out a navy in the Forth. When the English army set off for France – and a rapid victory – James' fleet sailed north and fell on Carrickfergus in English-dominated Ulster.

Unshaken, Henry landed his army in Flanders, scorned a Scots herald and sent the French packing. James assembled his horses and men.

Ghostly figures appeared at various Scottish towns, warning of impending calamity, but James ignored them, visiting his men on the Burgh Muir.

The Scots marched south, a huge army given at between 60000 and 100000. It was a large force by the standards of the time, and better equipped than many that had left Scotland. Artillery, one of James' pet loves, trundled under the command of Robert Borthwick, and before the clumsy, long-nosed cannon marched an army from all quarters of Scotland. Amongst the magnificence of the brave banners and trappings, men were already falling. Burgh Muir was Edinburgh's plague isolation area and the germs had struck at the army.

Crossing the Border, James wasted his army, in snatching half-a-dozen keeps, and his time, in paying court to Lady Heron of Ford Castle. In the meantime the English were marshalling their forces. Ten times the population of Scotland, England could gather an army equal in size to any of Scotland without weakening her main strength. Howard, Earl of Surrey, did so now. Marching to meet the Scottish threat, Surrey was joined by hard-riding Northumbrians. With the banner of St Cuthbert damply on its staff, Surrey was joined by Dacre and his Cumbrians at Newcastle and advanced on the dallying James.

A challenge was made and accepted and so the two armies were to meet on Friday 9 September 1513. In a rare mood of wisdom, James positioned his force perfectly, his pikes protecting the high ground of Monylaws and Flodden where Surrey would have to advance at a disadvantage. Staring at defeat, Surrey put on a display of bravado. 'Come and fight me in the open ground,' he offered, cynically letting the Scots throw away their superiority. However, James managed to retain his good sense; he stayed put but his anger was already rising.

With 1000 seamen reinforcing him, Surrey marched along the Till River to confront the Scots centre at Monylaws. Motionless, James watched, and continued to watch as Surrey withdrew again, his mailed men marching over Twizel Bridge. At this point James should have acted; Borthwick in charge of the artillery begged to fire, the Earl of Huntly wished to advance and Lindsay of the Byres was threatened with hanging for daring to suggest an attack while the English were disorganised. James was too chivalric to do any such thing.

Friday 9 September brought driving rain and James, finally and too late, moved. Surrey was beneath Branxton Bridge in two divisions, each in two parts. James advanced in five divisions, a long line of spears and swords. A few hours before sunset and the two armies faced each other, a quarter of a mile apart and with smoke from James' burning camp drifting and concealing. Until now the Scots still held the advantage of ground; if James had let Surrey come to him he might yet have won, but his spearmen, mauled by English artillery, moved forward. Borthwick was already dead, slain by a cannon ball as his own shots flew high.

Unused to standing to be slaughtered, Lord Home's left division of Borderers and men from Clan Gordon poured on to the English right and broke it in a few minutes of thrusting lance and hacking sword. Home continued his wild charge until he reached the English camp, when the natural instincts of the Borderers led them to plunder. Dacre led 1500 English on to them, there was a sharp mêlée which ended with Scots and English withdrawing and watching each other. Home's men took no further part in the action.

Both Scots central divisions slid down the grass towards the remaining three English divisions, hit a valley and dragged themselves a couple of hundred yards towards the waiting billmen. The lines met with all the fury of long-standing enemies and the Scots found that for once they were not winning the close quarter fight. The English bills had a long blade which sliced the point off the Scottish spears. The resulting long pole was useless and the Scots fought on with sticks, knives and swords. Again the English had the advantage of weapons and the Scots had to use courage as a shield.

James was in there, his sword hacking at English billmen as he strove to reach Surrey. Perforated by arrows, one hand near hacked off, James was within feet of Surrey before a bill decapitated him.

Of the two remaining Scots divisions, the reserve under Bothwell remained in position without moving, while Argyle's Highlanders were caught in flank by bowmen and an English charge. They scattered; Highland fighting did not demand heroic stands.

Stanley, who had broken the Highlanders, moved his men behind the now-surrounded Scots and a circle of steel gradually closed on the diminishing army. They fought with terrible courage and died on the bloody grass of Branxton. Some had removed their shoes to get a better grip; a poignant detail.

Ten thousand Scots died, including 13 earls. The English lost 1500 – or more, but it was the sad belief that four horsemen had carried away the King of Scots and led him to fight in the crusades that told the true loss of Flodden.

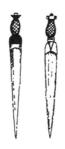

Hadden Rigg and Solway Moss

After Flodden, never again would a Scottish King command in a major encounter, not for three decades would a large Scottish army cross the Border. The lesson of Flodden was caution, the loss of thrusting leadership less grievous than the diminishing of martial élan. James IV was replaced by James V, an infant. Regents again ruled the land until James, a teenager at the time, escaped from guardians to snatch the reins of runaway Scotland.

For the reins required a restraining royal hand. James V faced a nation torn by internal strife and he stalked the Border rustlers with a noose, set King Campbell against the red sword of MacDonald. James accepted the Pope's title of 'Defender of the Faith' and milked gold from the abbeys to help maintain his dignity. He married twice and both times added the dowry to the bare coffers of Scotland.

From a good beginning the King slipped downhill. His twin lusts – money and women – irritated his volatile people and his policy of taking the lands of heirless nobles angered the Lords. Trouble in the Hebrides brought him west, and his refusal to back Argyle left his Campbells disgruntled. There was a parliament but the King listened only to the words of his favourites and spent the once-hoarded money of the nation on them and himself. The Scots did not love a spendthrift, vindictive monarch and their toleration, never strong, was stretched.

Unprepared and divided against itself, Scotland began to drift into yet another English war. Minor warfare was already endemic along the wind-whipped hills of the Cheviots.

In his demented pride, Henry VIII of England had thrust himself adrift from the Catholic mainstream of Europe and the Pope quickly called for a crusade. James, Defender of the Faith, showed he had some of his father's honour – and a fair share of his foolishness – by agreeing to participate. Unfortunately his allies, the Holy Roman Empire and France, preferred to bicker with each other and Scotland was forced to go it alone.

With the sense of timing the Stuart kings were famed

for, James decided to discuss matters with Henry in person, and in York. The Scots Privy Council were not pleased and showed touching loyalty when they forcibly restrained their King. Like most people, they did not trust Henry.

Justifiably annoyed with James' non-appearance, Henry could not control his mental instability. All the old emnities were recalled, all the hoary fabrications of English overlordship and soon Scotland was renewing her acquaintance with England by mutual piracy. True to their blood the Borderers of both nations harried everyone in sight, Scots pillaging Scots as willingly as crossing the frontier, and English helping on both sides of Cheviot. This was normal, but Bowes, the English East March Warden, possibly with the encouragement of Henry, took an army of 3000 into Scotland for revenge. Aided by the exiled Earl of Angus and his Douglas swords, Bowes brought fire and death to Teviotdale.

There was an established system to raids like this, and Bowes was conventional. Leaving his main force at Hadden, two detachments were ordered to rake the summer fields for booty; the principle here was for the smaller sections to lure an unsuspecting attacker into an ambush. Unfortunately for Bowes, the Scots were masters of these small-scale actions; it was in large battles that their generalship failed.

George Gordon, Earl of Huntly, waited until the foraying detachments, who were being led by Sir John Heron, were engrossed in their raiding, circled behind them and attacked. It was a neat little ambush of a couple of thousand men and the result was a running battle back to Bowes' force at Hadden. The Northumbrians were reported to have run first, more concerned with keeping their stolen cattle than fighting the Scots. When the mob of panicking Englishmen was herded towards him, Bowes did not know what to do; his carefully contrived plan did not allow for this and his ambush flopped completely.

Huntly, together with the Earl of Home and some 400 horsemen, scattered the English and the survivors fled to the Border. The Scots took about 600 prisoners, including Bowes and Heron. Perhaps 400 English died, making the raiders' casualties 30 per cent.

A traitor but no coward, the Earl of Angus stabbed one man to death with a dagger and escaped. His part in the frontier wars was not yet finished.

On 24 August 1542, as the battle of Hadden Rigg was decided, Henry called up his army. Twenty thousand Englishmen under the Earl of Norfolk crossed into Scotland in October. Wasting and destroying on his way, Norfolk marched up Tweeddale with Huntly's smaller force watching for its chance. After a week which saw twelve towns and two abbeys destroyed, Norfolk withdrew to Berwick.

By now James had an army ready and thrust it towards the Border, but the nobles would not fight for a despised King. They marched as far as Fala Moor, an exposed, barren place between Lauderdale and Lothian, and stopped. Why fight France's war? There was little food in November in the Borders, no comfort to be found among the heather hills. Why fight at all? This time James' arrogance had rebounded on him. Returning to Edinburgh, James found himself in the position of having to raise yet another force.

Unusually for a Stuart, James had a modicum of cunning, and he announced his intention of invading by the east, while preparing to strike at the west. Strangely, the English were completely fooled and Norfolk kept his 20000 in the flat lands near Berwick. Led by James and a Border expert, Lord Maxwell, the new Scots army of something more than 10000 men approached the extreme western end of the border. At Lochmaben James was struck by illness and the army marched without him to the Esk.

By now the English were aware of the threat. Wharton, the King's representative or Warden of the West March region, gathered the entire fighting strength of his area and advanced to meet the Scots. Three thousand Cumbrians against a royal army, but Wharton was as veteran as Maxwell. The Scots would have to negotiate the Solway Moss, a dank area of bogland and sinking sands, and as it was late November the ground would be soft and very wet.

They crossed the border at dawn on 24 November, 10000 Scots under Maxwell, and all England lay before them. Two hundred, maybe 300, light English horsemen were harassing their flanks, but the Cumbrians had only nuisance value and Maxwell would send his own Borderers to deal with them. On the banks of the Esk the army halted and Oliver Sinclair, one of the King's favourites, proclaimed he had been appointed to lead the army. There would have been consternation, as fighting men listened incredulously as the Royal Commission was read out. Maxwell would have cursed, men would have murmured in horror, drifted away away from the army, refused to fight for such a creature as Oliver Sinclair. And all the time the English horsemen were attacking the suddenly leaderless Scots.

Wharton threw his force at the disarrayed army. There was no resistance; hemmed between the Esk and the Moss and with only a panicking fool to command them, the Scots lost all desire to fight. Many surrendered in sheer disgust. Solway Moss was hardly a battle; the Scots surrendered, or ran into the Moss to get back home. The English, using only a few hundred men, lost seven killed, the Scots only 20 – and others drowned – but over 1000 prisoners were taken. Earls and lords were captured, Lord Maxwell himself and Oliver Sinclair.

And as the Scots scattered, the wild men of Liddesdale, themselves Scots, attacked the fleeing soldiers for fun and profit.

When James heard the news his first thought was for Oliver. 'Is Oliver taken? All is lost!' And, a few days later, he heard of the birth of his daughter, 'a vereye weyke childe', and then died shortly after.

Mary, Queen of Scots was born at Linlithgow on 7 December 1542.

Ancrum Moor and Pinkie

Fair Maiden Lilliard
Lies under this stane;
Little was her stature
But muckle was her fame.
Upon the English loons
She laid many thumps
And when her legs were cuttid off
She fought upon her stumps.

Fair Maiden Lilliard probably did not exist, but the Lilliard Stone is on the site of the battle of Ancrum Moor, one of the strangest of all the battles fought between Scots and English. It came at a crucial time in Scottish history and had an effect far greater than better-remembered encounters.

Since the rout of Solway Moss, Henry had been busy destroying Scotland. The Border was ablaze with Scots clans in English pay, and English fleets were ravaging both Clyde and Forth. Henry planned to marry his son to Mary who was still in infancy.

In order to convince the Scots of his intent he sent the Earl of Hertford north with concise instructions to make Edinburgh 'a perpetuel memory' not forgetting to be 'putting man, woman and childe to fyre and swoorde without exception'.

In 1544 Hertford did just that, but his 'Rough Wooing' did not have quite the required effect. Not unusually, the Scots nobles did not excel themselves and it was left to the citizens of Edinburgh to make the invaders fight through the wynds, where pikemen lunged from smoke-filled closes.

Apart from isolated skirmishes, Scots resistance was minimal and disjointed. A Scots army failed before Coldingham but the Earl of Angus, once in English service, performed heroics in rescuing endangered artillery and Bothwell bravely held the rearguard. The English rape of southern Scotland was a mistake. Where coercion might have worked, terror only bred resistance, and when Sir Ralph Eure was promised a royal grant of all the lands he subdued in the eastern borders, the Earl of Angus vowed revenge. 'I will witness the deeds,' Angus swore, 'on Eure's skin with sharp pens and bloody ink.' Eure's reply was to the point; 5000 mixed English, Scots and mercenaries destroyed the Douglas tomb at Melrose and burned the tower of Broomhouse with an elderly woman still inside.

With a following of 300 men, Angus rode into the bloodied Borderland to beard Sir Ralph and his savages. Surveying the shattered wreck of Melrose, Angus had to avoid an English night attack and slowly gathered reinforcements. Scott of Buccleuch rode in from Teviotdale and Lesley of Rothes with 1000 Fife riders. Under Angus' command they watched Eure and waited.

There were perhaps 1500 Scots, and Eure had 3000, but they were homeward bound, slack with greed and soft with easy raiding. Buccleuch advised the Scots to dismount on the moor at Ancrum, a few miles north of Jedburgh.

Buccleuch was a wily Border fighter and he set the Scots into an ambush position, with spears in a vicious hedge but hidden by a fold of ground. The camp-followers were sent to the rear leading the horses, so Eure, half-blinded by the slanting sun, thought all the Scots were running. Layton and Bowes led the vanguard, Eure led the main body. The English had spearmen in the centre, soldiers carrying hackbutts, or early firearms, and archers on either flank. When Angus' men rose to meet them the English could not halt in time. It is said that a heron flew between the armies just before they clashed and Angus bemoaned the lack of a hunting hawk.

Raw wind blasted smoke into English faces as the long Scottish spears jabbed the vanguard into a terri-fied retreat. However, the main body slammed onward, tearing itself into disarray on the Scots line. Renegade Scots riding for England chose this time to rip off the red cross of St George and turned coat again. The Turnbulls claim that this action of theirs won the battle. Easy to criticise, but if the Scots nobility – like Angus – could change sides, why not the ordinary clansmen?

When the slaughter ended the English had lost 800 dead and 1000 prisoners. As the survivors scattered, the persecuted folk of the Border took revenge.

The Earl of Arran, who had been constant on the Scots side, asked for God's mercy on Eure 'for he was a fell cruel man'. There had been no surrender for the likes of him. And Maiden Lilliard? Perhaps she fought at Ancrum, or chased the fleeing fugitives.

Ancrum Moor raised Scots morale and standing. A French force flitted through the Borders later in the year, but Henry was not finished with Scotland yet. 1545 saw another invasion with the English using foreign mercenaries and burning all they could find. There was a fierce fight at Kelso, a Scots counter-attack in the western hills and hatred generated from Solway to Dunbar. 1546 saw a brief peace, 1547 the death of Henry, but any hopes of peace were mistaken.

In autumn of 1547 the English came again: 18000 professionals who included 800 musketeers, 6000 cavalry and a detachment of Spanish mercenaries, on horseback and carrying carbineers. There were also 15 cannons and a supporting fleet. War-weary, impoverished but always defiant, Scotland gathered her men. Scotland sent forth the 'fiery cross'. This was a cross of hazel fired and quenched in the blood of a goat, and decked with a white rag. Thirty thousand men were pulled to this ancient symbol, ill-armed but prepared to fight. With the south a ravaged mess, most came from north of the Forth.

As the Duke of Somerset – once known as Hertford – led his army north, the Scots did little more than watch. Andrew Kerr of Ferniehurst attempted a delaying action at East Linton but was vastly outnumbered and the few cannon of Hailes Castle stuttered their fire at long range towards the steel-faced invaders.

The Earl of Arran commanded the main Scots host, the last time a feudal army fought for Scotland, and he brought it between Edinburgh and the English, thousands of footmen with the long spears which had won Bannockburn and Ancrum, lost Halidon and Flodden. Arran had some artillery, but not much, and to reply to Somerset's muskets he had a company of archers from Argyll. The Campbells were fixed in their loyalty.

A piece of foolishness on 9 September saw the entire Scots cavalry sucked into an unequal fight and destroyed in three hours of bloodshed. Wellington would have sympathised with Arran; his cavalry was a spent force soon after the start of Waterloo.

Next day, Black Saturday, as the English began to manoeuvre, Huntly challenged Somerset to a man-to-man contest. Somerset refused and marched towards his fleet in the sandy bay of Musselburgh.

Until now Arran held a strong position, with his spearmen in four great divisions and each flank covered; the right by a bog, the left by the Forth. Falside Hill overlooked the battle site and Somerset's cavalry trotted towards it. Angus aimed to get there first. A free race, cavalry against infantry and the cavalry won; they poured down from the north-sloping ridge and the Scots formed a spear ring. In the hedgehog formation of 18-foot-long spears, Scots infantry defeated English cavalry. But this was war, not a competition, and the English had their cannon and musketeers.

Spanish carbineers fought differently from English cavalry; they rode to pistol range, fired a volley and withdrew. The spearmen could not reach them and when artillery joined in, Angus' men began a slow withdrawal. On the other flank of the Scots, the English fleet had cannonaded the regiment of Argyll archers and these had left their position. Now they were round the spear ring, robbing the hundreds of speared cavalry and cutting a few throats.

When the cavalry came again, the Argyll men ran and Arran's main Scots army caught their panic. It was Solway Moss all over again but this time the English were looking for blood. When the stubborn spears began to drift away there was nothing to stop the English from killing. Ten thousand Scots died in the hideous chase, and 1500 prisoners were taken. It was the last full-scale battle between English and Scots and in the end no-one had won the long war. Scotland remained bloodied, broken but still fighting and even when England bought the disaffected and turned clan against clan, even with immense superiority in manpower and equipment, even with foreign mercenaries, Scotland did not surrender.

Within two years the last English army had left. Scotland had been helped by France but the merciless fighting which cleared the southern counties had been mainly carried out by Scots.

It was small-scale, ruthless fighting which the Scots excelled at and in the end won by. However, both countries had fought a hard, base war and both had lost.

CIVIL AND CLAN WARS

Red Harlaw

When not engaged in English wars, and often when they were, the Scots fought among themselves. This destructive feuding was every bit as ferocious as the national wars, and included major civil wars, clan warfare and the additional complication of Gaelic-cultured Highlanders fighting against 'civilised' Lowlanders.

The Highland fault line seems to be a natural barrier in Scotland, with the Gaels of the glens separated from the more taciturn Picts and Saxon-British of the coastal plains. This is an effect exaggerated by history. If the Scottish capital had been at Perth, as it often was, or near Oban, as it once was, the kings of the earlier centuries might have spread their Gaelic culture across the whole nation. But speculation cannot change facts; Highlander and Lowlander were destined to deviate and Clan Donald highlighted the difference.

MacDonald led the western Gael, the descendants of Dalriada and Somerled the Great. Perhaps their lifestyle, their legends and lore had as much of the Norseman as of their Ulster past, but in the days of MacDonald, Prince of the Isles, all Gaeldom looked to them for leadership. In 1263 Alexander III of Scotland fought off a Norwegian King from Scottish waters and reclaimed the Hebrides for himself. Alexander had not asked what the Hebrideans wanted and his successors had to cope with a people who wanted independence, a constant running sore in Scotland's flank. MacDonald of the Isles was the equal of any Lowland King, in the eyes of Clan Donald, and he held the Isles, from the Mull of Kintyre to the Butt of Lewis, as his own. He also held much of the western mainland and, two and a half centuries after a sea battle off Islay had founded his family, a prince of the Isles claimed the earldom of Ross.

This earldom stretched across northern Scotland from coast to coast, touching on fertile land too close to Inverness for the peace of Lowland minds. Donald of the Isles laid claim to Ross through Margaret, his wife, and her mother held the lands in her own right. There was another claim, that of a nun, Margaret's niece, Euphemia, but she had surrendered her right to John of Buchan on assuming the veil.

27

Raising an army, Donald swarmed across Scotland to take his inheritance – or was it a dowry?

Clan Donald was on the march, 10000 men – surely all the fighting strength of the Isles, if the figure was not swollen for effect. Men dressed in linen and smeared with pitch, with deerskin to blunt the blades of their enemies and broadswords with which to deal their own blows. Pipers would blast the glens with noise and their bows propelled arrows with a wicked barb, deadly to extract from their victim's body. Lochaber axes, curved and deadly, brass-bossed targets and the chiefs in chain with tartan plaid and swordhilts protruding above their left shoulders. Friend of the English King, Donald had blood in him as royal as Scotland's rulers and was bilingual, in English and Gaelic, and possibly spoke Latin and French as well. He was a man as educated as any at that time.

But if Donald was cultured, the man who would soon face him over the crossguard of a sword was not. Alexander, Earl of Mar, was a Stewart and closely related to both the Regent Albany and the rival claimant to Ross. Natural son of the late Wolf of Badenoch, this man took a wild band of Highlandmen to assault Kildrummie Castle, abduct the Countess of Mar and marry her to gain the title. Proving himself in continental warfare, Mar turned to piracy, scouring the coast of north-east England with a small fleet. With this chequered history, Mar seemed an excellent choice to halt the rampant Donald.

Mar gathered his men. There was popular Sir Alexander Irvine of Drum, Red Andrew Lesley of Balquhain, reputed father of 70 children – seven in one night! – Provost Davidson of Aberdeen with 36 brave citizens, Scrymgeour, hereditary Standard Bearer of Scotland. The lords and lairds of Mar, of the Garioch, of Angus and the Mearns donned their armour and sharpened the swords their fathers had worn.

They would have to be quick. Donald's galleys had carried the Islemen to the mainland and the clans had debouched eastward. But not all Highlanders tamely followed the Hebridean prince. The Mackays, under Angus Dhu, challenged him at Dingwall and there was a savage swordfight which ended with the Mackay chief captured and his warriors dead or in flight. By July Donald was in Inverness, with the local clans augmenting his force, and then began the march south and east.

The fair province of Moray was first to suffer as Islesmen and Highlanders swept through like a flame, then came Strathbogie and Mar's own lands of the Garioch. Rumours of Donald's intentions spread through the coastal Lowlands. Aberdeen was to be plundered, and all the fertile lands north of Tay. In this north-eastern shoulder of Scotland the Gael was the enemy, for English armies seldom penetrated past the buffer of the Borderland; fear of the Highlandman was widespread.

Leaving Aberdeen, Mar marched his mailed men, maybe 1000 strong, by Inverurie to meet Donald's might. Donald was waiting for him at the hamlet of Harlaw, bare mossland stretching from the River Urie north, with the lantern-height of Bennachie's 'mither-tap' or hill to the west. At dawn on 24 July 1411, Mar split his army in two; the men of Angus led with Scrymgeour and Sheriff Ogilvie in command. Behind came Mar and the family strengths of Irvines and Morays, Lesleys, Stirlings and Lovels, all the power of Aberdeenshire and the Mearns with their banners, horses and lances.

The Gaelic army was camped on a flat-topped hill and Scrymgeour brought his phalanx of armoured men to it, forestalling the terrifying Highland charge. There were no manoeuvres, just the onslaught of mailed men-at-arms into the deerskin and linen of the clans and at first the Lowlands pressed back the Gael. Heavy sword and battle-axe, mace and long Lowland spear, Scrymgeour cleaved a bloody path to the crest of the hill. There he stopped, with the men of Angus around him. Under Red Hector MacLean, the clans had rallied; instead of matching steel for steel with armoured men they equalised the Lowland advantage.

Nimble men darted beneath the great chargers of the knights, dirks sliced hamstrings and there was a sudden clatter as metal-clad men fell. The Angus men were driven back pace by pace as two opposing cultures fought for an earldom and died for a way of life. A Gaelic Scotland north of Tay or the Stewart power secure.

Mar was in a similar position to Scrymgeour, his advance slowed, his men hauled from their horses and dirked through their visors. Continental wars were gentlemanly compared to this slaughter, but

Mar struggled on and merged his force with the leading division.

Scrymgeour was slain; scion of a fighting family, the claymores had cleft him. Provost Davidson was dead, and most of his fighting Burghers around him. Lesley of Balquhain had also been slain and lay with six of his sons at his side. The Sheriff of Angus had died, and others, hundreds of others, as the Lowlanders formed a desperate ring and faced the courage of the Isles.

Red Hector MacLean fought and killed Alexander Irvine of Drum, but in killing was himself killed. The chief of Mackintosh lay dead, Captain of Clan Chattan, and only darkness ended the battle. It had seen the Lowlanders at their best, as dour defenders, and Highlanders as the swift-charging light infantry. There was no apparent victor.

Donald's clans drifted away. MacDonald, MacLean, MacLeod, Mackintosh, MacPherson, the septs of Clan Chattan, fierce hounds of Cameron – all had fought with all their strength and left 900 of their dead on the Red field of Harlaw. Bards would proclaim victory and they would be right; for they had certainly killed the best of the Lowlands. Six hundred of Mar's men had died, in spite of their armour.

And the earldom of Ross? Regent Albany gave it to his son.

Bloody Bay

North of Tobermory in the Island of Mull is Rubha nan Gall, or the Point of the Stranger, and a lighthouse blinks its message of danger to all seafarers from the Sound of Mull to the southern shore of the Ardnamurchan peninsula. Above the point the coast sheers into the indentation of Bloody Bay, with its isolated columns of basalt and hard-grained sandstone. This is a quiet place, save for the endless suck of the sea and the sway of forest firs – only the birds break the silence, and the thump of a tourist's boot. Once, though, it was different. For one day in the closing decades of the fifteenth century the future of a lordship was decided in this place and the Hebrides saw a family dispute settled with the sea churned by the oars of a hundred galleys.

In 1480 Clan Donald still ruled unchallenged in the western sea. From his castle in Loch Finlaggan in Islay, the Lord of the Isles ordered his people in Scotland and the Antrim Glens of Ulster, and the King of England and of Scots would speak with Clan Donald and beg an alliance. If the kings of Scots did not quite agree with this view, the bards of Clan Donald did, as they saw the world from a Hebridean viewpoint; the mainland was a peripheral zone. When the Isles engaged in warfare with James III, the Scots termed it rebellion, the Isles a legitimate war.

For centuries the Scots kings had tried to subdue their western seaboard. Diplomacy and force had both been tried but Clan Donald's grip had never weakened. The only solution was to divide and conquer but now the Isles were splitting of their own accord. Angus Og of the Isles had revived a claim for the earldom of Ross and his followers had surged east. Inverness was torched, a royal force under the Earl of Atholl defeated at Lagebraad in Ross and Angus seemed supreme.

But there was a slight difficulty, a rival to the lordship. This was the current Lord, John of the Isles, father of Angus and a man with a following. No enemy of the King, John had taken Ross from Angus, his son out of wedlock, and had granted lands of his lordship to other clans. Kintyre and Knapdale had been given away, and this made John unpopular, for that area of southern Argyll was the MacDonald heartland, home of

31

Somerled. Clan Donald gave its loyalty to the clan as a whole, withdrew it from the ageing chief. Support for John came from the vassal clans, the MacLeans of Mull and Harris, MacLeods of Skye and MacNeils of Barra.

· James III was not the warrior his son was to prove and instead of leading an expedition himself, he ordered his earls to quell Angus. This time there were two earls involved: Atholl again, backed by the Campbell Earl of Argyle. At this time the Campbells were not the terrifying power of later centuries but were still the Highland arm of the crown. Augmenting the earl's strength was John of the Isles and his associated clans. With a three-pronged attack, Angus Og was clearly in trouble.

However, neither of the earls pursued their offensive and John was left to reconquer the Hebrides without their help. Filled with pride of race, John did his best. An islander, he chose the western sea as his battleground and the Hebridean galley as both transport and weapon.

Descended from the Viking longboat, the Hebridean galley, or lymphad, was a fast fighting ship which had been clinker-built and had a platform at bow and stern. Other medieval craft had these platforms which were named forecastle and aftcastle, but lacked the galley's speed. With two dozen oars of pine and two or three men for each oar, plus a section of purely fighting men, these vessels could carry 100 men at a pinch. The greatest chiefs of Clan Donald commanded over 100 vessels, including the smaller 16-oared birlinns, or chief's barges. With a rudder to steer by, a square lug-sail and the clan crest flaunted by flags and banners, a fleet of galleys would be an impressive sight.

John arranged a rendezvous at the bay north of Tobermory in Mull and waited there as his followers slowly gathered. It would be a tense time as galley after galley surged through the blue swell, pennants stiff in the Hebridean wind, crews cheering as they joined the assembled fleet. It is not known exactly when they met but it was probably late in the year.

But while John was mustering his strength, Angus Og was not far away. North of Mull the great peninsula of Ardnamurchan points a rocky finger at the Western Isles. It is a wild place, speckled with castles and on the northern shore was Angus Og. Perhaps he was in Sanna Bay, perhaps slightly to the east, but the cadet clans of Donald swung beside his war-galley.

Storm-bound for five weeks, Angus Og's Mac-Donalds began to run short of food. Ardnamurchan was a poor place to support an army, and there would have been scores of galleys there. The crews, dressed in linen and deerskin, would have been avidly watching the weather for change. At last, the wind abated. Adverse weather conditions were still present but no longer a storm. Angus led his fleet along the coast of Ardnamurchan and round the point into the Sound of Mull.

There Angus found a single galley. As Angus' fleet appeared, line after line of swift ships, the galley ran up her colours. MacLean of Ardgour had come to join John's fleet. There was no hesitation from Clan Donald; with oars thrashing the blue-green water, Angus launched himself at Ardgour.

Seeing Ardgour attacked, the craft of MacLean of Duart, kinsman of Ardgour and captain of John's fleet, surged to his aid. MacLeod of Harris followed at his stern and MacNeil of Barra, perhaps the most unruly of all the island clans, swooped into battle. With these three heroes committed, the other galleys joined in.

The galleys carried archers with the short Highland bow and the wide-barbed arrow, but the main tactic was to grapple and board. As the leadership would be aft, on the sterncastle, this would be the prime target for attack. Ranald Bain MacDonald threw his grappling irons at MacLeod of Harris' vessel and the swordsmen of Clan Donald leapt aboard. Edmund More Obrien proved his courage by jamming an oar between MacLeod's rudder and sternpost so the galley could not be steered.

As this struggle continued, multiplied five score by the tight fleets, Angus Og faced MacLean of Duart in person. With Allan of Mudort, Angus captured the Mullman and prepared to hang him from the mast of his own galley, but Mudort laughed this off. 'No, Angus,' he said, uncoiling the hempen collar, 'if Duart is dead, who would you have to squabble with?'

William Dubh MacLeod, an old man now, was killed and when Ranald Bain took the galley of MacLeod of Lewis, the heir to the chief was found wounded, with two arrows deep in his body. The heir died later, on his way to Dunvegan in Skye. All over the bay, the blades of Clan Donald were victorious and seeing this, MacNeil of Barra fled for his own castle of Kismuil. Although three MacDonald galleys chased him, MacNeil had the skill to escape by dodging nimbly round Coll. He was lucky – the sea of the bay was swirling red with the blood of Hebridean clansmen that day.

Far away to the south a single galley, Campbell colours flapping, slipped from Argyll. The Earl of Atholl was aboard and he crossed to Islay to kidnap Donald Dhu, Angus' son. But in spite of this Angus held on to his gains. For the rest of his life, Angus was Lord of the Isles, but he was to be the last.

The title was forfeited to the crown by James IV and thereafter the history of the clans was to be one of fragmentation.

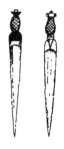

Langside

Her name has come tripping down the centuries as the epitome of romance, her reputation that of a tragic beauty. Was she a pawn of ruthless men or a calculating player on the power board of international politics? It was the misfortune of Mary, Queen of Scots, to be born at a time of traumatic change, to lose her father when only a few days old and to aspire to the Scots crown when active men were ranged in opposition. Poor Mary – her aura haunts a dozen Scots castles for her life was full of misery and shattered hope.

Born in Scotland but raised in France, she married the doomed Dauphin, later to become Francis II. The world thought her beautiful but deadly. She was considered a threat to England by her presence, to Scotland by her religion. Her landing at Leith was masked by mist, her homecoming to Holyrood spoiled by singers. Mary had to contend with opposition by John Knox at his most vehement and a Protestant population afire with newly converted zeal. Mary also had her admirers and a Catholic support in and out of Scotland.

An ill-timed rebellion ended in activity as Mary helped flush the rebels from the tumbled hills of the south. Beside her rode full-blooded James Hepburn, Earl of Bothwell. The vicious murder of Rizzio her servant in her presence and the threats of the Earl of Ruthven caused the pregnant Queen to make for Dunbar from where she returned with loyal thousands. All her reign she was on the defensive, forgiving one group of enemies and making another. When her second husband Lord Darnley died under suspicious circumstances in an Edinburgh bomb-blast (or more probably, by a strangler's hands since the body was unmarked) Mary needed more friends than she had.

Condemned guilty by whispered rumour, innocent by trial, Bothwell remained close to the Queen. Too close, for he kidnapped her near Cramond, drove her to Dunbar and into muddled matrimony. Murder was bad enough but this was worse. Lord Home camped out-side Bothwell's twin-towered turret of Borthwick, south of Dalkeith, and Mary had to climb from a window, dressed as a boy. With a few hundred men she faced the Lords of the Congregation at Carberry Hill. Neither side had many warriors, neither wanted to fight, but the rebels had Kirkcaldy of Grange and fighting Ruthven. As her army diminished by desertion, Mary surrendered.

Bothwell slipped away to the Northern Isles, pur-sued by Kirkcaldy of Grange. He finally ended up in a Scandinavian prison. He died years later, chained to a pillar, a madman who had once married a queen.

Forced to abdicate, and imprisoned in Loch Leven Castle, Mary miscarried Bothwell's child. Another catastrophe in her sad life. She encountered a spark of light as she escaped from Loch Leven Castle aided by loyal George Douglas. Other lords were still willing to fight for their Queen – two centuries later a Bonnie Prince, equally tragic, would inspire equal devotion – Lord Seton, Lord Claud Hamilton, Lord Livingstone, Robert Melville, Johnnie Maxwell of Herries.

They met at Hamilton Castle, decided that Regent Moray, Mary's brother, was the enemy and sent a mes-sage to France for help.

Men were drawn to Mary's banner and the prospect of a fight. The Campbells came south from their Argyll glens, their claymores joining the Hamilton spearmen and loose lances of the border. Kerrs of Ferniehirst came up from Teviotdale and the Annandale Johnsons joined their hereditary Maxwell enemies to fight for Mary.

Mary was only 25 at this time – the same age as the Culloden combatants – and foolish enough to choose a poor general. The Earl of Argyle led the royal army, an epileptic distantly related to Mary through marriage. This unfortunate choice of general estranged Claud

Hamilton; however, ill-feeling was nothing new among Mary's men.

There was more hope: Huntly, Cock of the North, was coming south with Gordon reinforcements, Lord Fleming waited at the rock fortress of Dumbarton with more. At the head of her quarrelling army of 6000, Mary headed for Dumbarton.

Based in the small town of Glasgow, Moray aimed at interception. His own force was slowly sinking as men deserted to Mary, so he sent for reinforcements. The Earls of Morton, Glencairn and Lennox marched their men to him, Mar sent cannon and warriors, Home kept a Hepburn from taking Dunbar Castle and brought 600 horsemen from the Merse, Edinburgh found volunteers and armed them with hagbuts — the rifles of the day. Four thousand men gathered in Glasgow, at their head Kirkcaldy of Grange. With a European reputation and the best general in Scotland, he took charge of the regent's army.

Kirkcaldy selected the site for battle; the hamlet of Langside, south of Glasgow and near the moor of Govan. Fording the Clyde, Kirkcaldy had his cavalry dismount and wait in ambush at Langside. They waited there, attempting to keep their slowmatches sheltered from the driving rain as Moray and Morton displayed their main might on the banks of the Clyde.

Hoping his vanguard were covered by the ten cannon on Clancart Hill, Lord Claud Hamilton advanced them, 2000 strong, through Langside village. Kirkcaldy's hagbutters had their chance. Amidst the smoke and stench of burning powder, Hamilton's men were splintered. At first they fell back but then rallied and drove on. Each cottage was a strong point, each dyke sheltered a marksman, but the Hamiltons were stubborn.

Withdrawing before such numbers, the hagbutters had torn bloody holes in Mary's vanguard. Panting uphill, the Hamiltons met the van of Moray's army, long pikes on their shoulders and with Kirkcaldy in command. Hamilton hesitated; there was a cavalry battle on the flanks and cannonballs striking amongst his men. His losses had already been severe but Lord Claud was as brave as he was loyal and ordered his pikes levelled. This was a push of pike with a vengeance. Two horizontal walls of long spears, light glinting on wet wood and no chinks between the intertwined poles.

Impasse at the head of the hamlet, but elsewhere the battle was turning in Mary's favour. The hope which had sparked at the shore of Loch Leven must have flared into life as the right flank of Moray's army began to tremble. There was hard fighting here. Home, bleeding from more than one wound, was unhorsed but rescued by Walter Kerr of Cessford, while the other branch of the Kerr clan lunged desperately at Moray's men. Outnumbered, the regent's cavalry scattered, but Kirkcaldy charged in with reinforcements.

With this sudden onslaught, Mary's line held firm but Argyle's did not. The Campbell earl, brother-in-law to Moray, slid from his horse in a fit of epilepsy or treason. Leaderless, the royal army recoiled, and Moray sent in his Highlanders. The Macfarlanes, to whom Campbell was no friend, bounded at their prey. The Hamilton spearmen joined the rout.

It had taken three-quarters of an hour to extinguish the smoulder of Mary's hope. From now she would know only flight and captivity, with the English Queen, Elizabeth, soon to be a captor cousin. There was one last, cynical twist to the tale: in Scotland two castles held for the Queen, Dumbarton and Edinburgh.

Defender of Edinburgh for many years was Kirkcaldy of Grange, the same man who had shattered Mary's advantage at Langside.

RELIGIOUS WARS

Inverlochy

When Jenny Geddes lifted her stool and hurled it at the minister in grey St Giles, she could have had little idea that the ensuing violence would climax with war in all four of Britain's countries and only end when a dark and bitter King stepped ashore from foreign exile. If she had known, Jenny might not have yelled 'Daur ye cry mass in my lug?' Jenny, and people like her, caused a series of wars which made countries tremble and caused a King to lose first his crown and then his head.

For the Reformed Church was becoming ever more militant and was dividing into contending factions. Religion was to remain an issue in British political thought for centuries to come. While Europe bled with the Thirty Years War, and Scots mercenaries filled the ranks in the Swedish army, Scots at home listened in disbelief as a London-based King proposed to change their Kirk. Charles Stuart intended to alter the Scots Church to align with Anglican practices.

Scotland replied with the National Covenant and the Covenanters were born. It seems to be a common occurrence in Scottish history for the people to declare their opposition by a democratically drawn-up document, signed by thousands. This version had copies distributed around the country and caused feelings to rise against all but the Presbyterian religion. Those Episcopalian bishops who had domiciled in Scotland quietly slipped south. As Charles raised militiamen in northern England, the Covenanters claimed they were not against the King in person, but mustered their men nevertheless.

The King planned three assaults on the country of his blood: two set off; one failed to land in the Forth and the other was outfaced by blue-bonneted Covenanters at Duns. In Aberdeenshire a young man, James Graham, Marquis of Montrose, trotted the Gordon royalists out of Turriff and the banner of the Covenant waved secure. One year later, 1640, and crooked Alexander Leslie led the blue bonnets over the border, whiffed away a royalist force at Newark and forced Charles Stuart into conflict with his English parliament.

But the Covenant had sworn to defend the King and the signatories began to disagree. Montrose remained true to his word and his monarch. Others did not. As religious war smouldered in Ireland and civil war flared in England, Archibald Campbell, Earl of Argyle – Gruamach the Sullen to some – rose to prominence among the more extreme Solemn League and Covenanters. Presbyterian Scots armies fought to defend their co-religionists in Ulster. A Scots Division won Marston Moor for Cromwell, garrisoned the English north for parliament and Highland 'redshanks' clashed with Covenanters in the west.

As Leslie and Argyle held Scotland for the Covenanters, Montrose begged Prince Rupert for 1000 men to win back the nation. Rupert refused, the King gave a title instead and Montrose became a Lieutenant General who had to raise his own army to conquer Scotland for another man. The Lowlands were solidly for the Covenant so Montrose looked to the Highlands for help. Fifteen hundred mixed Ulstermen of Clan Donald and MacLeans of Mull rallied to him, but that was less important than the man who led them.

Alasdair MacColla MacDonald was a fighting man with a reputation. Veteran of the Ulster wars, he was a hero of Clan Donald and was to be a villain of Lowland Scotland. Alasdair was the focal figure for the western clans to follow, Montrose merely a Lowland lord who sometimes helped. Their enemy was King Campbell.

Joining Montrose and Alasdair was an amalgamation of Atholl clans and they met the Covenanters on the field of Tippermuir by Perth. On 1 September 1644 the royalist army hurled rocks in lieu of bullets and charged twice their numbers to begin a series of victories that was to lift Montrose to the status of military genius and split Lowland sympathies from the Stuarts forever. Then followed a roundabout march to Aberdeen, another victory, this time against burghers and farming people who did not know how to fight. Wild clansmen descended upon Aberdeen.

The sack of Aberdeen stained Montrose's honour and turned opinion hard away from a royalist army which acted so savagely. Stripping and killing, raping and robbing, women were kidnapped and carried away, Highlanders and Ulstermen alike became reviled.

When Argyle raised 4000 men and hurried to gain revenge, Montrose forced his disintegrating army to weave away among the autumn hills.

Alasdair MacColla brought more men from the clans of the western Highlands who hated the Campbells, and Argyle slipped back to his heartland. Winter closed the campaigning season, but not for Montrose. Perhaps he wanted his rear secure, or wanted to pursue his personal feud with Argyle, but he led his army over the snow-choked passes into the Campbell lands and began to spoil the glens and homesteads of the Campbells. When the allied clans were finished, they claimed that no cock crowed and no chimney smoked within 20 miles of Inveraray, Argyle's capital.

Montrose left for Inverness, but the Covenanters proved they could raise clans too, and all the Mackenzie might barred the Great Glen. With Lowland levies marching against him, and Argyle bringing 3000 at his back, Montrose appeared to be trapped. But he had 1500 fighting Gaels, Alasdair and the pipes and he forced them into a circuitous clamber which brought them level with the Campbells at a place and time totally unexpected to Argyle.

South of the Great Glen is Glen Tarff and the Car Leac pass, deep in snow and dangerous with avalanches and driving sleet in winter. In the bitter white of a Highland winter, Montrose trudged through Glen Roy and the torrents of a sudden thaw, clashed with unlucky Campbells and then descended from the harsh flank of Ben Nevis to the bleak levels of Inverlochy.

The Covenanters had become aware of their approach and hastily prepared for battle. It was the dawn of 2 February 1645 and the Covenanters were led by Sir Duncan Campbell of Auchinbreck, an Ulster veteran whose lands Montrose had destroyed. He had over 1000 Lowland infantry under two colonels, probably a mixture of pikemen and musketeers, but militia, not regulars. On either side of the Lowlanders were 1000 Campbells, traditionally armed with bows and arrows, axes, broadswords and a few muskets. Two cannon gave artillery support more in theory than fact, while the extreme left of Auchinbreck's line was secured by 50 musketeers in Inverlochy Castle. Argyle, obviously considering himself too valuable to risk, watched proceedings from a galley in Loch Linnhe.

To oppose this, Montrose put his Ulstermen on both flanks commanded by Alasdair and Manus O'Cahan respectively. His centre was purely Highland, Appin and Atholl Stewarts, Camerons and Glencoe MacDonalds for a vanguard, supported by various septs of Clan Donald and MacLean. Before the battle there was prayer, to St Patrick and St Bride, the latter being a sanctified remnant of an old pre-Christian Celtic deity – and immediately afterwards the killing began.

Unconventional in his manoeuvring, Montrose attacked in a style to become traditional among Highland armies. His entire line advanced towards the Campbells, discharged their firearms and the flanks charged, closely followed by the centre.

To the Lowlanders it was a terrible sight. Sudden smoke and flame and a leaping, bounding array of screaming savages, broadswords upraised, targes held to cover bowed heads and dirks gripped in left hands. The original lines became grouped together as the Highlanders closed and formed wedges – Bruce's army used this technique, and Napoleon's infantry on a slower, grander scale.

Probably only armed with pikes and definitely undertrained to face such a method of warfare, the Lowlanders broke. It was not suprising; their pikemen could hardly be expected to face a whirling yard of steel which could slice them in two. Their departure left the Campbells vulnerable and Montrose's men closed with them. Although still outnumbering the royalists, the Campbells were forced back, fighting desperately. They fought for their homes and families; there were scores to pay on both sides but Clan Donald were the more experienced. The Campbells ran.

Some ran to the castle and were hewn down outside the walls, others were killed running, or drowned in swollen rivers. Perhaps half the Covenanting army died – certainly there was no quarter for the Campbells. Equally certain, Argyle slipped away in his galley.

Montrose had other victories to come, but to his Highland following Inverlochy was the important one. The power of the Campbells had been broken and it was a Lowland army which eventually defeated Montrose, a Lowland army which hunted Alasdair Mac Colla down the length of Kintyre. Fighting for his King, Montrose was betrayed by a Highlandman and hanged in Edinburgh. A few years later Argyle was beheaded in the same city and today both lie in Jenny Geddes' Kirk of St Giles, separated in death by the width of the building as they were separated in life by their ideals.

Drumclog and Bothwell Brig

The latter half of the 17th century was remarkable for the alternating fortunes of the politico-religious rulers. First Charles held power, then Cromwell, another Charles, a James and a William. Charles II, misnamed the Merrie Monarch, gave his word to stand firm by the Scottish Covenanters, accepted the Scots throne at Scone and promptly lost a battle and his kingdom. He returned on the death of Cromwell, broke his royal oath and imposed bishops on the Scots Kirk, dragoons on the Covenanting counties of the south-west.

Years had changed the Covenanters, no earl or marquis wrecked the solidarity of their peasant ranks and the spontaneous rising of 1666 was led by a mere colonel. Three thousand men armed with pitchforks and staffs left the west, 1000 remained when they glowered on the tenements of Edinburgh and withdrew to face the dragoons on a Pentland slope. The Covenanters stood three charges before they broke and were eventually defeated. The survivors were hanged and transported for bonded slaves to the West Indies.

Lang Tam Dalyell had crushed the rising, and he and his followers harried the stubborn peasants of the Covenanting west. The Presbyterians met at secret religious meetings, or conventicles in the hills with a circle of musketmen around to ward off the dragoons. There were many bloody skirmishes on the bare lowland hills.

This was the time of legends, of Dalyell's fun in throwing women into pits full of snakes, of men hanged on their own door lintels. These peasants were tenants and their lairds were held responsible for them. All conventicles were to be broken up and any landowner who refused to help could be fined; instead of turning master against man, this forged links of shared suffering.

As the conventicles continued, the government became desperate. Highlanders were recruited and for three months of 1678 a Highland Host – reinforced by Lowland troops – occupied Ayrshire. A year later the Covenanters replied with violence: Archbishop Sharp was murdered at Magus Muir in Fife; armed men felled him and killed him by crushing his skull while his daughter watched. This action marked an obvious point of no return.

A huge conventicle was arranged for the end of May, somewhere in Lanarkshire. This was more than a gesture of defiance, it was a challenge that the government had to meet to retain credibility. John Graham of Claverhouse was sent to find and disband the meeting; he left Glasgow on the last day of May. Claverhouse was young and eager, and had not yet earned his nickname of 'Bloody Clavers' or the reputation of rolling prisoners downhill in barrels full of spikes. He was a captain of the King though, and took 15 prisoners in Hamilton for interrogation. One of these saintly Covenanters was the Reverend King, famed for his preaching but not for his morals; he had been sacked as Lord Cardross' personal chaplain because of a 'misadventure with a maidservant'.

Either King or another informed Claverhouse that the conventicle was to be held the following day at Loudon Hill, a spot already used by Wallace and Bruce for ambushes. Undeterred, or uncaring, Claverhouse dumped his prisoners at Strathaven and went over the moor to Loudon. About 250 lifeguards and dragoons jingled behind him, enough redcoats and sabres to scatter any number of ragged muirmen, those who came from the heaths and moors.

Climbing Loudon, an isolated, eerie mound in the central Ayrshire plain, the gallant captain saw about 1500 Covenanters about half a mile to the north. They did not seem to look at all terrified of the scarlet soldiers coming towards them. Deciding to parley, Claverhouse sent a man forward.

Robert Hamilton was the head Covenanter, and he ordered all women, children and the elderly to the rear while all fit men advanced in a rough line. To the professional troops it would be a laughable sight as the countrymen shambled forward, singing the psalm to the tune 'The Martyrs' and clutching a motley collection of pitchforks and other warlike implements.

There was a bog – one of many – on the Covenanting flank and Claverhouse sent a small party to surround it. The dragoons had the advantage of it being the Sabbath; some of the Covenanters would not defile a Sunday by fighting, so they withdrew instead. Others were more martial and remained. William Cleland brought up a group of dedicated men. Pitchforks and scythes against curved swords, it was an easy victory for Claverhouse.

Cleland waited until the troopers were deep in the bog and then lunged at their flank.

Ploughing through the marsh, the cavalry had no advantage and were outnumbered. Pitchfork and flail, scythe and pike, the Covenanters had degenerated from the proud blue bonnets who had followed Leslie and fought at Marston Moor. But so had the royal army. With 30 of his men dead, Claverhouse was forced to withdraw; he had lost the battle of Drumclog. His own sorrel horse was hurt, pierced by the pike of Rab Fleming.

A brief exchange of swords with Cleland, and Claverhouse ran. One man had fired eight shots at the captain; each one missed.

Claverhouse withdrew to Glasgow, leaving his dead to be mutilated, his wounded to be shot. But even Glasgow was not safe as the Covenanters came on in force, attacking hastily erected barricades at the Gallowgate and the Cross, Tolbooth and College. Powder smoke and psalms until both sides recoiled and Claverhouse collected himself at Falkirk.

It was now full-scale civil war, with the militia mobilised and armed men guarding the fords of Forth. There was panic spreading among the government but already the tide had turned; the Covenanters began to argue among themselves.

Troubles in the east saw a scattering of Covenanters near Selkirk but the main effort was always in the west. Sixteen days after Drumclog, the Covenanters clustered at Rutherglen ready to attack anybody, especially dragoons and bishops. Dragoons the government had — four more troops were despatched to Scotland, and the King sent his son, James, Duke of Monmouth, to command. On 19 June, Monmouth took over the army and advanced into the hostile west.

Just north of Hamilton a bridge crossed the Clyde and at Bothwell Bridge the Covenanters made their stand. Between them and Monmouth's force of perhaps 2000 the Clyde acted as a moat and Bothwell Bridge was the only crossing. With 5000 men David Hackston of Rathillet could be optimistic; he knew his infantry could be trusted, of the cavalry he was not so sure. John Balfour of Kinloch led them, while Hackston barricaded the bridge, said a prayer or two and waited. It was Sunday 22 June: the Reverend Welsh preached and the Covenanters polished their single bronze cannon hopefully.

Monmouth had more artillery with which he commenced a cannonade. Quite happy in the memory of Drumclog, the Covenanters opened their last bag of powder to find it held raisins. Now they could do little but suffer – or parley. They treated with the enemy for a while and then resumed the fight. Either Hackston used the truce to purchase more powder, or the psalm-singing worked a miracle, for the raisin-ammunition of the Covenanters drove Monmouth's artillerymen from their cannon.

The skill of the professional soldiers began to tell. When the Covenanters fire lagged, footguards thundered on to the stone-arched bridge. Musketry and Balfour's cavalry ran, but the infantry, the backbone of any Scots army, fought grimly. The ragged men with broad bonnets and homespuns exchanged blows with hardened guardsmen, but when Claverhouse brought over his dragoons the Covenanters had little chance. Hackston's men fought, and it was not until the cannon tore holes in their ranks that they broke.

Twelve hundred were captured, but many were butchered on the battlefield and in the pursuit. Strangely, it was Monmouth who spoke for the prisoners and many survived by agreeing not to rebel again. Two hundred refused, and most of them died on their way to the American plantations. In the west, the killing time started in earnest, with Covenanting extremists following a Richard Cameron and Claverhouse earning his reputation. Like Monmouth and Cleland, these men would be remembered in times to come.

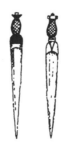

JACOBITE WARS

Killiecrankie

When Charles II died, James ascended the throne. The seventh King of Scots to bear that name, and the second to rule all Britain, James' Catholicism brought swift rebellion from Argyle. Again the head of Clan Campbell was separated from his body, again Clan Donald wasted the glens of Argyll. Religious feelings ran too high in Britain for James' gestures of equality to be accepted; for in Scotland the Presbyterians were still outlawed.

It could not last. In 1688 Dutch William was invited to take the crown and one-third of his military credentials were Scots as he landed at Torbay and marched on London. Through William's wife, Mary, there was still Scots blood on the throne, albeit diluted, and more Scots welcomed William than opposed him. However, no Scots minority is ever keen to submit to new authority and the north was in ferment.

Hardliners of both sides came forward. The Covenanting west rose for William, threw out all vestiges of episcopacy and headed for Edinburgh in a body. The capital was in chaos as the Estates decided which dynasty should rule, aided on one side by a Protestant mob and three regiments, on the other by Claverhouse, now Viscount Dundee, and 50 horsemen. There was no contest: Dundee slipped out of the castle by a postern gate and galloped to the Highland line.

A nation in turmoil, the rival factions recoiled to consider strategy. Edinburgh Castle, holding for James, was blockaded while new regiments were raised from the Edinburgh streets. The Earl of Angus called together the Covenanters, named them Cameronians after a martyred preacher, and gave command to William Cleland, veteran of Drumclog and Bothwell. The Earl of Leven did even better: descended from Alexander Leslie of Newark fame, he drummed up 800 volunteers in two hours and had them in ranks by the grey abbey of Holyrood. Hugh Mackay of Scourie, a mercenary who had been abroad all his fighting life, took command in Scotland. He performed a lightning march north to view the Highlands before returning south for reinforcements.

Dundee had ridden north and west, gathering what clans were willing to fight for James – or against Argyle. Out of all the strength of the Highlands he could raise 2000 men: Clanranald, MacDonalds, Camerons, MacLeans and Stewarts, MacDonald of the Isles and of Glengarry. He also had a few hundred Irish and a mounted body of Jacobite lairds – and some of the dragoons who had been harrying the Covenanters.

Toward the end of July Dundee led his clansmen south to Atholl and began the siege of Blair Atholl Castle. Mackay marched to Perth, Dunkeld and northward to meet Dundee's army. Mackay, the Highlander, commanded a Lowland army of around 4000: the ex-Dutch regiments of Ramsay's, Balfour's and Mackay's; Hasting's regiment, Leven's newly raised foot and a body of levies under Viscount Kenmore. He also had some horse, about 100 under Lords Belhaven and Armadale. As Mackay reached the foot of the pass through Killiecrankie, Dundee was just north of the head.

In this period the best men of the infantry were formed into 'fusilier' companies, the élite of the army, and Mackay sent a couple of hundred of these to hold the northern end of the pass. Two miles in length and overlooked by wooded heights, the Pass of Killiecrankie was a ferocious defile for an army to enter, ready made for ambushes. There was no road, just a rough track which had never been furrowed by the wheels of a wagon, and it is said that one of Mackay's continental troops refused to enter such a terrible place. At ten in the morning of 27 July 1689, Mackay began to thread through the pass. Two hundred of Leven's regiment marched in front to reinforce the fusiliers, and the rest, together with 1200 baggage horses, slipped and slithered above the Garry River.

There was no ambush in the pass and only one casualty, a craftsman shot by a Highland sniper. If Dundee had held the pass in force, history could have been changed; as it was, he only had a few Highlanders on the heights to attack stragglers.

Through the pass there was level ground and a field of yellow corn; the infantry waited for the baggage to catch up. Again the fusiliers acted as vanguard – and found the Highland army. By the time Mackay reached the front the Jacobite Highlanders were in position. On high ground and in clan regiments, the Jacobites had the Royal Stuart standard of James VII on display. They looked down on the redcoats, waiting.

Mackay had all the time in the world to order his

force. The fusiliers held a wooded knoll to the left, line regiments arranged three deep with each battalion split in two. One pikeman to every five muskets and the musketmen with a plug bayonet, fitting into the muzzle of their musket, to repel a charge. Mackay left a gap between each battalion, a tempting hole in the centre of his line. Behind this hole in their defence his cavalry waited for the order to charge.

Aware that a large number of his men were inexperienced and none had fought Highlanders, Mackay encouraged them with a speech and warned that there could be no retreat, for the local Athollmen would enjoy killing redcoats.

In the meantime, Dundee was waiting. Occasionally one of his men sniped at Mackay, or the Lowlanders fired their three leather cannon, but the time was not yet right. For two hours the Jacobites did nothing, and when they did move, it was hardly inspiring. The sun was dipping when the Highlanders moved slowly forward.

It was not a flood of tartan for the plaids had been discarded; they came in their shirts, barefoot and some barechested. They carried Lochaber axes and dirks, steel pistols made in Doune and Dundee. They held the yard-long broadsword, baskethilted and double-edged. Some had flintlock muskets. At their head, against the advice of Cameron of Lochiel, was Dundee and his horsemen. He must have remembered a similar advance ten years before at Drumclog.

'Fire by platoons,' the redcoats were ordered, 'at 100 paces.' A spattering of shots came from the Highlanders, causing a man to drop here and there. The advance quickened as the clans neared their enemy. Then the high battle-cries, slogans of the Gael, sounded out, firearms fell and out come the swords and the advance changed to a full charge. One volley of fire from the redcoats and hundreds fell from the side of the attackers. The Lowlanders were now struggling to plug in their bayonets. The Highlanders reached them. Most redcoats fled at the sight of thousands of yard-long swords wielded by screaming Gaels, whilst others were cut down in droves. Only the right of the line held where the pikes of Hastings' and Leven's regiment stabbed at Bullhide and broadsword. The remainder of the redcoats fled, for these veterans from Flanders could not face the Gael. The fusiliers ran, Colonel Balfour of Balfour's regiment was killed and as Mackay tried to force his cavalry to take the Highlanders in flank, they fled too.

Joining Leven's and Hastings' foot, Mackay withdrew to Stirling, picking up strays from Ramsay's on the way. The government army had been defeated but the Jacobites had lost too. Dundee, leading the charge, had been shot through the breastplate. Nobody saw him die, but his cause had lost its leader and would never recover.

About 800 Highlanders died that day, and only 400 redcoats survived. Those who died, died horribly. For many of the fallen had been decapitated, sliced in two, skulls cloven to the breastbone; such was the power of a Highland broadsword. There was no pursuit of the redcoats, for the Jacobites were busy plundering the baggage train.

Colonel Cannon took over the Highland army and led them to Dunkeld. Here he met the new Cameronian regiment under Cleland. Entrenched, the Cameronians slogged it out for three hours, finally fighting with the town burning behind them and lighted faggots on the points of their own pikes. As the Highlanders charged again, the Cameronians rose from their trenches and heaved them back by push of pike.

Three hundred Highlanders did not return, but the Cameronians' psalm of praise was muted, for William Cleland was among their slain.

As the Scottish war petered out and the focus of attention moved to Ireland, General Mackay pondered what had gone wrong. He invented a bayonet which would fit round the rim of the musket-muzzle. Next time, the clans would not catch his redcoats at a disadvantage.

Sherrifmuir

Since the revolution which put William on the throne, Scotland had slumbered uneasily. The battles of the 1689 rising had been followed by years of terrible famine. An attempt to create a colony in Central America ended in diseased disaster with only a shred of pride in a victorious jungle battle. The English Union of 1707 brought despair, hardship and loss of industry and pride. Taxation and poverty destroyed Scotland's assets and people looked back to a supposed golden age when a Stuart King sat secure on a Scots throne.

Support for the Stuarts was less strong than detestation of the Union, and the plans for a rising in 1708 depended largely on a French fleet that was turned back in the Firth of Forth. Nevertheless, the government responded by arresting many and disaffection with the Union became a unifying force between Gael and Lowlander.

In 1714 George I ascended the British throne; known as a 'German Lairdie' to Jacobite propagandists, movements began to bring back the Stuarts. It was quarter of a century since James VII had left the country and a generation had grown to manhood without knowing the destruction of civil war.

'Bobbing John' Erskine, Earl of Mar, was chosen to lead the next Jacobite rising. His nickname was well-earned, for he moved from one political side to another whenever the grass looked greener. It was on his lands, on 6 September 1715, that the standard on the Braes o' Mar was raised, and the audience was small but hopeful. The government army was equally small but less hopeful. General Wightman had around 1000 men to hold down all Scotland – so he sent for reinforcements. Two regiments of dragoons came up from the north of England, one of dragoons and two of foot from Ireland. Even better news for the government: French support, vital to the rising, was not forthcoming.

Frightened of the memory of Killiecrankie, the government sent the Duke of Argyle to Scotland to take over from Wightman. Argyle was a veteran of Marlborough's wars and quickly organised his forces. Three volunteer battalions were raised in Glasgow, led by Colonel Blackadder who had fought with the Cameronians at

Dunkeld. Now with over 2000 men under his command, Argyle felt safer, but still needed more.

Meanwhile, the Jacobites were busy. An attempt on Edinburgh Castle narrowly failed, as did an attack on Inverlochy. Western clans, under Russian veteran General Gordon, marched east and the MacGregors raided along Lochlomondside. There were also other connected risings. Mackintosh of Borlum crossed the Forth in a fleet of small boats, frightened Edinburgh and marched south to join Jacobite groups in the Borders and Northumberland. After a period of disagreement and countermarching, the combined force entered England and held Preston against a government army. It took a determined attack by the government Cameronians and flanking assaults by cavalry to defeat them. The Englishman in command of the Jacobites, Thomas Forster, surrendered the whole force.

The main effort, however, was in the north. The Earl of Mar occupied Perth until all that were coming had come, and with an army of around 8000 men he headed for Stirling and the Forth crossings. Dunblane was the initial objective, where the rounded Ochil Hills slipped into the plain of Forth, but Argyle had learned of the plan.

Little more than 3000 redcoats followed Argyle as he left Stirling on Saturday 12 November. He had 1000 cavalry and 2000 foot; some were very inexperienced but others were veterans of European battles. At this time the redcoats had a European reputation of toughness and discipline which the soldiers had gained on the marches of Marlborough. This discipline was ferocious, the individual soldier tough. Once a man joined the British army there was no way out except death, desertion or disbandment; there were no terms of enlistment. All he had to do was fight – and he did.

Two hours before dawn on Sunday 13 November 1715 the Jacobites left their quarters and assembled for the coming battle. In two lines on the frosty grass, the Jacobites could not see Argyle's army, but a small party of cavalry was watching them. Mar sent a body of horses to scare off the watchers, then he discovered exactly where Argyle's force was formed and moved against them. Argyle waited on the braes above Dunblane until the Jacobites advanced, then marched to find a better position.

The redcoats wanted to make Mar charge uphill to

them, but moved into position too slowly. The left and centre left of the government army was badly spaced out as the Highlanders crested the white ridge of Sherrifmuir within easy charging distance.

General Gordon led the right wing of the Jacobites, and ordered them to attack the redcoats. Up against infantry and dragoons, the Highlanders advanced, firing a single volley, they dropped as the redcoats returned fire and then charged. However, the Captain of Clanranald was shot down, causing his men to falter. 'Revenge!' demanded MacDonald of Glengarry, rallying them, and Clan Donald responded. Four minutes after the order, they were hacking at the frenzied lines of infantry.

Since Killiecrankie, British infantry had been rearmed; they used a bayonet which fitted round the muzzle of their musket and had discarded all pikemen. This meant there were more musketmen in a battalion, more fire-power. Trained to stand three deep and fire volleys by platoon, they had time for only one shot each before the broadswords and spiked shields of Mar's men were among them.

Bayonet against sword, the redcoat infantry was forced back until they were fighting in their own second line, and then until they were mixed with the dragoons. After a frantic minute of terror, when they were confronted with blood-greased blades and the screeching voices from Highland faces, the redcoats broke ranks. The entire right wing of Argyle's army fled in panic, with clansmen chasing, killing, massacring. The Jacobites gave no quarter, breaking into groups to pursue their prey, butchering redcoats in the heather, on the banks of the Wharry Burn, wherever they could. Arriving in Stirling, exhausted redcoats reported the defeat of Argyle's army. They were wrong.

Back on Sherrifmuir, the Jacobite cavalry, 1000 men strong, assembled on the Hill of Kippendavie. From here they watched, but did nothing as the left flank of their army charged three redcoat battalions under Argyle himself. The 25th infantry was here, now known as Shannon's; it had been termed Leven's when it held firm at Killiecrankie. Against this regiment, with its supporting battalions, the Highland charge faltered, and Argyle sent his cavalry to smash the Jacobite flank.

Royal Scots Greys and the dragoons attacked the Jacobites, there ensued a partial withdrawal and then the Highlanders reformed. After a dozen cavalry attacks and three hours of fighting, Mar's left flank was three miles back at the Allan Water.

Both armies had achieved some success, but when Argyle reached the Allan Water he learned of the disaster to his left flank and withdrew to reform. About 1000 redcoats, including the Grey cavalry, waited behind the poor cover of mud walls as Mar collected his scattered Highlanders and advanced. Four hundred yards from Argyle, the Jacobites halted; they outnumbered their enemy by four to one but their cavalry was suspect. For half an hour the armies faced each other but Mar did nothing. At dusk he withdrew. The Jacobite chance had been squandered.

A ballad summed the whole affair in simple, scathing terms:

A battle there was that I saw man,
And we ran, and they ran,
And they ran, and we ran,
And we ran, and they ran awa' man.

But that battle decided the rising. Argyle had nearly 700 casualties, Mar only 232, but he had failed to cross the Forth. When James did arrive in Scotland, he was too late. His short tour of the north was not successful and his orders to burn villages in front of Argyle's army damaged his reputation and caused suffering to his people.

There were few regrets when he left, and the stage was cleared for his son, Charlie the Young Pretender, to act his part.

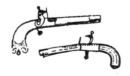

Prestonpans

Thirty years had passed since Sherrifmuir and Scotland
had drifted from thoughts of a Stuart King. There was a
little more money in the land, a few more ships trad-
ing from ports in Clyde, Forth and up the east coast.
Smuggling was endemic, the last witch had been burned
and the double-crossed flag of the Union hung sullenly
secure from royal garrisons throughout the land.

In the Lowlands there were muted gestures of defiance; a toast to the 'King over the Water', drunk by
passing two fingers above the claret glass – although
there was less claret now, due to the French wars.

Where the Lowlands met the hills, Clan Gregor was
still outlawed. The Black Watch, first of many Highland
regiments, had been formed. For the Gaelic heart still
beat strongly, with only minor signs that the arteries were
beginning to harden.

If there had not been a rising in 1745 the clan system would have lasted longer. However, it would still
have died with the advent of progress. So it was to a
doomed society that Prince Charles Edward Stuart, son
of James the Old Pretender and grandson of a king, sailed
from France. The last and arguably the most famous
Stuart landed on the tiny island of Eriskay, and was
advised to return. Unwanted, Charles hit the mainland
at Moidart with seven advisers and began his search for
loyal clansmen.

Surprisingly, they came. Not quickly, not en masse,
but a thin trickle of western Highlanders. All the old
federation of Clan Donald were asked, a few arrived.
MacDonald of Clanranald sent his son, MacDonald of
Keppoch; Lochiel brought his fierce Camerons and the
Mull MacLeans left their island. Even the MacGregors,
proscribed or not, sent a contingent from Balquhidder.
Most of these Highland militia were not volunteers, but
ordinary men from the communal farms of the glens
and if they disobeyed their chief's command they could
have been evicted, or awakened to find flames licking
at their thatch. Press-ganged into fighting, the clansmen
were feared already and under the Young Chevalier
their reputation was to rise to unprecedented heights.
Victories lay before them, and a deeper penetration of
England than any previous army of Scotsmen.

They did not fight for Scotland, but to put a Stuart King on the British throne. That was the official line, but the clansmen had little interest in events beyond Tweed and Cheviot, much more in their own Highlands. Their weapons and tactics remained basically unchanged from those their forefathers used fighting for Montrose: the flintlock volley, the claymore charge, the unnerving yell. Ferocity and reputation fought for them; that and their own courage, their undoubted skill with the sword.

Of the men who led them much has been written to obscure the truth behind a patina of romance. Prince Charles had pawned his jewellery to finance his expedition. Undoubtedly charming, his real feelings for the clansmen were less admirable than his reputation. Decked in tartan, Charles declared that he needed only 'the itch' to feel a real Highlander.

Lord George Murray, second in command of the Jacobites, has been lauded as an excellent general whose advice should have been followed and might have led to success. Lord George was also the man who fired the villages after Sherrifmuir and who proposed destroying the crops of deserters. The deserters were from his own people; an intriguing side of the Jacobite's chivalry and one which highlights the individual bravery of the Highlander even more.

Clanranald, chief of his branch of Clan Donald, sent his son to fight for him; other chiefs joined only when success seemed possible. Lochiel was probably the most loyal supporter the Stuarts had; he brought 700 of his Camerons – by threats as much as promises.

The initial moves of the Jacobites possessed a dynamism unseen since Dundee's demise. When the redcoat army of General Cope tramped north to trap the clans in their glens, Charles evaded it with ease and took Perth. Here, the old capital of Scotland, James VIII was declared King and the tartaned clans hurried south. There were fords beyond Stirling and the populated plain of Forth empty of defenders.

A skirmish brought Charles Edinburgh, although the castle held solid beneath its crossed union banner, and cheering crowds called to the clans. All Scotland seemed to belong to Charlie, yet Johnnie Cope had sailed from Aberdeen and was ordering his army in East Lothian.

Johnnie Cope was an experienced general and he had 3000 men to command. As usual the redcoats were a mixture of veterans and untried recruits. The regiments were still named after their colonels: Lee, Lascelles, Murray. They fought in line and marched in column as their fathers had done at Sherrifmuir and Malplaquet. They sported scarlet and tricorn hats, mitre caps and spatterdash, or long-legged gaiters. Each man held a Brown Bess musket and bayonet, had powdered hair tight in a braid and feared the lash. They marched to the tuck of a drum and the sweetness of a fife; fought for their regiment and for drink.

With an army of something less than 2000 men, Charles left the capital to challenge Cope. The redcoats were against the shore of the Forth, fully aware of Charlie's army and prepared to receive the Highlanders with grapeshot, with volley fire and dragoons. There was only one approach to Cope's men, from the south, and levelled muskets had that covered.

The clans would have to rely on a frontal charge – effective, but as demonstrated at Killiecrankie, costly. They had to find another way. They discovered there was an alternative. A local Jacobite guided the Highlanders round the flank of Cope's army. This entailed a night march through a marsh, with the knowledge of thousands of the enemy very close.

21 September 1745 and the mist from the Forth clung damp to the coastal plains. The redcoats waited at the salt pans of Preston, but Charlie was beyond them. The Jacobites advanced in two lines, 50 yards apart and silent until they were seen. Numb and tired, Cope's sentries yelled a warning and only then did Highland slogans rant high above the screen of mist.

Pandemonium broke out among the regulars. The dragoons struggled to find their horses, infantrymen fumbled for their muskets, artillery men wrestled round their cannon to face the onslaught; they had as little chance as they had time. The first line of clansmen arrived armed with broadswords and Lochaber axes, dirks and the battle-lust of the Gael. Redcoats were cut down and slaughtered. Resistance collapsed almost immediately amidst the panic and terror, and the victorious Highland cheers.

General Cope tried his best. With his charger hurt, bleeding from the swing of a Lochaber axe, Cope yelled frantic orders to his dragoons, tried to rally them, to make them counter-charge the Jacobites. He failed; British regulars broke and ran before the charge of Highland militia. Before the second line of Jacobites, some armed only with scythes, could take part in the battle, the fighting was over. Five minutes of fighting decided Prestonpans, ten minutes of killing and taking prisoners completed the victory of the Bonnie Prince. Charlie had conquered Scotland.

There was also booty: tents, cannon, standards and, when the Jacobite officers halted the killing, 1500 prisoners. Among them was one David Gordon, an officer of Lascelles; his great-grandson was Charles 'Chinese' Gordon of Khartoum. One casually swung broadsword could have altered history for thousands of people in China and the Sudan.

Charlie waited a month in Edinburgh before deciding to march into England. His army had been strengthened by more of Clan Donald, by MacGregors, by Appin Stewarts and MacPhersons, by Robertsons and men of Atholl. Avoiding the gathering government armies, Charlie moved south. In November he took Carlisle and hoped for English recruits; he got a few hundred Mancunians. On 4 December he reached Derby and was advised to withdraw.

The peak had been reached. Two redcoat armies, both larger than his, manoeuvred to catch him. At Clifton, Murray defeated Cumberland, and at Falkirk Charlie defeated Hawley and the redcoats scattered. With redcoats gathered from Flanders, the Campbells rose for the government and Charlie withdrew further and further north. At Inverness he heard that Cumberland, who was marching against him, was at Nairn.

Charles Edward Stuart decided on a night march.

Culloden

The two unequal armies of volunteers and conscripts faced each other across the width of Drummossie's boggy moor. They were brave men but fearful, dressed in scarlet uniforms and tartan philabegs. Above the wind and rain rose the war-pipes of the Gael and the rolling drumbeat of the regulars.

For Cumberland's redcoats it was a good site for a battle: level enough to watch the enemy approach, level enough to decimate them by volley fire in the manner of Flanders. Some had fought at Fontenoy and faced the French. Since Falkirk they had been retrained to face a Highland charge; and so ignore attacks to their front and bayonet Highlanders attacking to their right. Government artillery waited with grapeshot and solid iron ball.

For the Jacobites it was a poor day for battle. They had been marching and fighting for months and for two days and nights continuously. The night before they had marched as far as Nairn to surprise Cumberland's army, but without success. They had eaten almost nothing that day, and the day before. Exhausted and hungry, they assembled with their clansmen, faces to the sleet, and watched as the redcoats unfurled before them, dragging out the artillery.

To fight these redcoats the Highlanders would have to close to a sword length; to do that they would have to undergo an advance under cannonade and musketry, in full daylight against an army twice their size.

There were 8800 redcoats, including artillery and the Campbells. The Jacobites numbered about 4500 including redcoat deserters, old men and unarmed children.

Midmorning of Wednesday 16 April 1746 and the Duke of Cumberland, 25 years old, ordered the slaughter to begin. Trained artillerymen fired ten cannon at will, the smoke jetting and rolling, lying thick and high on the heather to hide both armies. Three-pound balls of iron struck the unprotected men of Highland glen and Hebridean island. At Waterloo, Wellington ordered his regulars to retire behind a ridge and lie down before the enemy cannonade; at Culloden, the Jacobite officers ordered their desperately tired militia to close ranks and form a better target. There were only a few Jacobite guns, no trained gunners, no backup and after nine minutes firing, no more gunfire to support the Stuarts.

Falling and dying, standing among the dead and mutilated wounded they had always known, the Highlanders clamoured for the command to charge. There was dismay in their ranks, dismay among the MacDonalds who had been posted on the left, not the right which had been their prerogative since Bannockburn. Dismay at the lack of food, at the choice of battlefield, at their mounting casualties. They stood in two lines, a front line – including, from left to right, MacDonalds, Stewarts, Farquharsons, Chattan, Frasers, Appin clans and the Camerons. Behind the front line were various detachments of Franco-Scots and Franco-Irish Lowlanders, men of little experience and no good in the attack. They were of little use in the only sort of battle the Highlanders could fight.

Opposite, hidden by powder smoke, Cumberland's army waited as their enemies were reduced minute by minute. There were three Scots Lowland regiments among the redcoats, Royal Scots, oldest of all British line regiments, the Scots Fusiliers and the 25th Foot who had fought at Killiecrankie and Sherrifmuir. There was a battalion of Campbells and more Campbells as scouts and irregulars.

Campbells trotted round the Jacobite flank, opened the way for 500 dragoons to attack. To oppose them, Charlie had a handful of cavalry, but a deep ditch was a more effective defence.

'Claymore' was the order which would send the clans bounding forward, but it had not come when the advance began. No co-ordinated attack by the entire line, no attempt to pierce a weak point in the redcoat ranks, only a rush forward caused by the frustration of taking casualties without reply. The confederated clans of Chattan drove forward first, into the grapeshot and musket-hail, and the Camerons and Appin Stewarts followed, then the men of Atholl, so the whole Jacobite right was in motion.

They ran into the grapeshot and into the musketry of six regiments of regular soldiers. The survivors faced three ranks of lunging bayonets. Some even broke through them.

Too angry to fire the single volley which could have weakened the government infantry, the clansmen ran

upon men unbroken, into aimed musketry, into blast-
ing cannon, and died. Some stopped to throw stones.
Some stood yards away, yelling in defiant impotence
and were shot by laughing musketeers. The few who
broke through the front line battalions died on the steel
bayonets of the second.

A redcoat eye-witness reported that the Highlanders
shouted 'Run ye dogs' as they charged. If individual calls
could be heard above the clamour of battle, they would
certainly have been in Gaelic as the clans fought for their
way of life.

Camerons and Stewarts broke through the ranks of
Munros and Barrells foot and at last the Highlanders
could retaliate. It was a terrible struggle, with redcoat
platoons breaking to run, but flanking fire from Wolfe
– hero of the Heights of Abraham – and the Campbells,
by Sempill's 25th, halted the Highlanders.

After the cannonade and the muskets, the bayonets
and flanking volleys, the surviving Jacobites could do
no more. Gradually they began to drift back, still with
musketry slicing into them. The Campbells on their flank
fired more volleys and charged with the broadsword;
the 500 dragoons leapt on the retreating clans.

The Campbells were fought to a standstill, dragoons
held by 60 ill-horsed cavalry, but the battle was already
lost.

On the left, Clan Donald advanced. They had 600
yards to cover and were under fire the whole time. They
did not reach the bayonets. Before Clan Donald was
within range of the red soldiers they stopped, attempting
to lure their enemy forward. It did not work; instead the

regulars aimed and fired at this static target. There was no hope for Clan Donald and they died in droves before retreating.

As the Highlanders ran, their despised second line closed to cover. Franco-Irish and Franco-Scots held back the butchering dragoons before themselves withdrawing. They left behind them a moor choked with the dead of the clans. The exact number of their dead is uncertain – around 1200 or 2000. They had been killed for a Prince who would leave them to suffer. The government admitted to a total of 50 dead, 259 wounded – conservative figures, as the clans broke through two regiments and fought back in their retreat.

With the battle won, the killing continued. All the bloodlust of frustrated men, of men who had run in terror from Highland broadswords at Falkirk, who lived in fear of the lash and gallows noose, was set free. There was no mercy shown to wounded clansmen, or to innocent bystanders. Cumberland earned his nickname of 'Butcher' as his army terrorised the glens for months after.

Rape was common, torture approved, hanging and shooting applauded. Innocent and guilty alike were harried, babies spitted for fun. It was open season on the Gael as the Highlands were taught not to support a Stuart Prince.

The Prince escaped, £30000 in gold on his head but the impoverished clansmen had more honour than greed. Charlie died abroad, a drunken clown who boasted of his youth, who had caused the death of thousands.

Culloden was the last battle fought in Scotland and probably the most bitterly remembered. For the regular regiments involved do not carry the honour of their colours and the moor is still haunted by the suffering of that day.

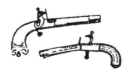

OVER THE FORTH

Over the Forth

The downslide of Imperial Britain coincided with the rise of Imperial Germany. As so often before, Europe clustered into armed camps and a local disturbance in the Balkans escalated into world war. On one side Britain, France and Russia, on the other Germany, Austria-Hungary and Turkey; four years of carnage left Europe exhausted, the old order shattered. Scots had fought in all theatres; 100 000 had died.

The First World War had weakened Britain; it had also introduced a new dimension to warfare. Now as well as battling on land and at sea, man could fight in the air. Dream or nightmare, it was a reality the major powers had to face and as Europe rearmed for the next round, air power was central to their strategy. With control of the air, generals could destroy armies, sink ships, demolish cities: or so the airmen claimed.

New types of aircraft rolled from their inventor's genius and slipped into the skies. Biplanes and monoplanes, fighters and bombers, Germany seemed to hold the initiative with their Messerschmitts, Junkers and Heinkels, but late in the 1930s Britain produced the Hurricane and Spitfire; time, blood and skill would decide which were the better machines. However, there was one drawback: relatively few British squadrons had these modern aircraft.

The Admiralty, naturally, had their own ideas about winning any forthcoming war. Fast ships and firepower forced the Germans to stay in port. Battleships were still the pride of the fleet with aircraft carriers a close second. The battlecruiser *Hood* was the Royal Navy's reply to a revived German fleet and she had similar status to the great *Michael* of James IV, or Nelson's *Victory*. The only problem about flagships was their vulnerability; the enemy always wanted to sink them. Hitler saw HMS *Hood* as a prime morale-boosting target.

So when war did inevitably break out, this time with Poland as the excuse, the German airforce, the Luftwaffe, searched for *Hood*. On 26 September 1939, a Luftwaffe patrol over the North Sea found her; the Dorniers also found the rest of the British Home Fleet. The carrier *Ark Royal*, battleships *Nelson* and *Rodney*, battlecruisers *Hood* and *Renown* and 13 attendant

warships: a quarry too good to ignore. Thirteen bombers were sent to attack the fleet, nine Heinkels, four
Junkers 88s. The aircraft attacked through an escort-
ing sheet of anti-aircraft fire but failed to sink anything,
despite extravagant claims.

The hunt continued. A combined Luftwaffe and Navy
operation on 9 October did not even find the Royal
Navy, yet alone sink any warships, and it was not
for another week that *Hood* was sighted again. Early
in the morning of 16 October, a reconnaissance aircraft droned high above the Forth. Below was the
Bass Rock, the islets of Inchkeith and Inchcolm, blue-
smoked Edinburgh and the orange cantilevers of the
Forth Bridge. More important was the huge battlecruiser
flattening the chopped waves. HMS *Hood* had been
found, butting towards the naval base of Rosyth.

Radio waves crackled as the German operator sent
home the news. Here was *Hood*, ready to be attacked
– but the Luftwaffe would have to be quick; orders for-
bade the attacking of any vessel in harbour. The war
was still in its early stages and neither side wanted to be
the first to cause civilian casualties. Or perhaps the Germans, remembering the First World War, were reluctant
to invite RAF retaliation.

Twelve Junkers 88s of Number One Squadron
Kampfgeschwader 30 (Eagle Wing) left Germany at
eleven in the morning. Apart from anti-aircraft fire,
Helmuth Pohle, commanding officer, expected little
resistance. The Junkers 88 was one of the fastest
bombers in the world, with a speed of 270 mph it
was as fast as many fighters. Certainly superior to the
Gloster Gladiators that were all 603 (City of Edinburgh)
Squadron was reported to fly.

Not that there was anything wrong with the Gladiator.
Its four Brownings and extreme manoeuvrability were
to take a toll of the enemy in Norway and Malta. 603
Squadron were Auxiliaries, the Air Force equivalent of
the Territorial Army.

To assist the anti-aircraft fire from *Hood* and other
ships, the 94th City of Edinburgh anti-aircraft regiment
had one 1917 three-inch gun and a few Lewis machine-
guns of around the same vintage. These were based on
Portobello Power Station and the Ramsay Technical
College.

In an hour and a quarter Number One Squadron was
over the Forth, so careless of 603's Gladiators that they

failed to adopt a fighting formation. There was a little flak but at 13000 feet Pohle felt secure; he searched for *Hood*. The Luftwaffe was too late: *Hood* was safe in Rosyth. But there were other targets for the aircraft: two cruisers, *Southampton* and *Edinburgh* and the destroyer *Mohawk*. The Junkers tilted into a dive.

All the warship's anti-aircraft defences were in action, perforating the autumn sky with shrapnel and smoke, but the German pilots were courageous. At an angle of 80 degrees they screamed down; flak hit the leading aircraft, destroying the cockpit escape hatch. Pohle gave a sharp order and seconds later a thousand-pound bomb crunched into HMS *Southampton*. The bomb penetrated three decks but destroyed only the Admiral's barge. *Edinburgh* and *Mohawk* were also hit but without major damage.

'Gin ye Daur', snarled 603 Squadron as its aircraft sped from Turnhouse. And 603 did not fly alone; 602 (City of Glasgow) Squadron joined them. A combined Scottish nemesis for the Luftwaffe. German intelligence had been wrong, for 603 Squadron had just taken delivery of Spitfires to replace their ageing Gladiators.

Pohle's leading Junkers was first to be hit as it recovered from the bombing dive. The rear-gunner tried to match the Spitfires' eight machine-guns, failed, and pieces of aircraft splintered and drifted toward the Forth.

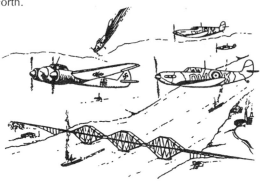

It was the first time the Spitfires had been in action, weekend pilots facing the best of Germany's bombers. But until now the Luftwaffe had only fought outmoded Polish aircraft. These Spitfires were piloted by names which were soon to become famous — Stevens, Sandy Johnstone, Denholm.